Simon Clarke

in company

Pre-intermediate

Unit and topics	Communication skills and tasks	Reading and listening texts	Grammar and Lexis links	
1 Selling your company p4 Company life Company descriptions Dot.com start-ups	Completing a report Discussing ideas for dot.com start-ups Preparing a web page	R Web page: the elevator pitch L Someone describing his company in 60 seconds R Report: Moonpig R Web page: betterdogfood.com	Present Simple Present Continuous	Business & the Internet
2 Women in business p10 Company life Work routines Stress & exercise	Identifying answers for questions Asking about work routines Asking about frequency Completing a questionnaire on exercise & stress Discussing exercise & ways to relax	R Web page: careers&women.com L Conversation: people talking about someone's job R Article on stress & exercise	Expressing frequency	Work & routines
3 Telephone talk p15 Connecting Using the telephone Telephone frustrations	Identifying telephone skills from telephone language Completing a questionnaire on telephone frustrations Asking indirect questions Telephoning for information & taking notes	L Saying numbers in words R Magazine article: *Ringing in the millions* L Conversation: checking flight details L Conversation: telephoning for an estimate	Indirect questions	On the telephone
4 Networking p20 Conversation skills Asking questions Making small talk Talking about other people	Constructing questions to use in conversation Putting a conversation in order Roleplays: talking about other people	L Two conversations: people meeting by chance on business trips L Conversation about a business contact		
5 Company histories p23 Company life Talking about the past	Asking questions about the past Doing a quiz about the Internet Asking questions using prompts Asking questions with no subject Preparing a web page with company information	R Company history: Nintendo L Radio documentary: the history of Nintendo L Radio documentary: the birth of the Internet R Magazine article: *Birth of the Internet*	Past Simple Time expressions *in*, *on*, *at*, *ago*, *when*	Business verbs
6 Correspondence p28 Connecting Methods of communication On-the-spot decisions	Discussing the advantages & disadvantages of communication methods & summarising results Solving problems quickly Recreating a conversation from prompts Putting a conversation in order Writing an e-mail from prompts Roleplay	R Magazine article: *Does grammar matter?* L Conversation: a request L Conversation: on-the-spot decisions L Conversations (x3): an important order	*Will* for unplanned decisions	Business communication
7 Making comparisons p33 Company life Comparing hotels & cars	Recreating a conversation from prompts Comparing two sports cars Comparing hotels & car manufacturers Discussing options for acquiring a hotel Ordering room service	L Conversation: at a hotel reception R Magazine article: *Hotel chain takeover* L Conversation: ordering room service	Comparatives & superlatives *As* or *than*	Hotel services
8 Did I ever tell you …? p38 Conversation skills Telling anecdotes	Making sentences from prompts Using *did* for emphasis Telling an anecdote from prompts	L Anecdote L Extracts from anecdotes L Using *did* for emphasis		
9 Spirit of enterprise p40 Company life Entrepreneurs Change	Putting a summary in order Recreating a conversation from prompts Describing change Finding out about a company	L Conversation between a bank manager & an entrepreneur L Interview: worm farm entrepreneur R Business briefing: Inditex	Present Perfect Present Perfect vs Past Simple	Word building
10 Stressed to the limit p44 Work issues Work-related stress	Discussing what factors produce stress at work Describing people's jobs using *have to* Making recommendations using *should* Writing a report on a company with problems	L Interviews: people talking about work-related stress R Magazine article: *Stressed to the limit*	*Have to, should* Giving advice using *should(n't)*	Stress at work

Unit and topics	Communication skills and tasks	Reading and listening texts	Grammar and Lexis links	
11 Top jobs p49 Company life Company history A top job Headhunting	Describing a company using the Present Perfect Asking questions with *How long ...?* Interviewing & writing a report	R Company history: Shimano L Radio profile: Steve Ballmer L Conversation: the headhunter	Present perfect – the unfinished past *Since & for; from ... to ...* *How long ...?*	Company news
12 Conversation gambits p54 Conversation skills Starting & leaving conversations	Introducing yourself Starting a conversation Deciding on 'safe' topics for conversation Saying goodbye/leaving a conversation Starting & maintaining a conversation	R Magazine article: *Remote Lounge* L Introductions at a conference L Conversation (in four parts): two people meet by chance in a bar		
13 Air travel p58 Connecting Conditions & consequences Negotiating	Completing a conversation Using conditionals with *will* Negotiating	L Conversation: at check-in L Advice on getting a good seat on a flight R Magazine article on air rage L Negotiating a deal	Conditionals with *will*	Negotiating & air travel
14 Hiring and firing p62 Work issues Losing your job Applying for a job A job interview	Using the passive to complete a report & rephrase facts Discussing when sacking is justified Identifying approaches to applying for a job Discussing workers' rights	R Newspaper article: a sacking L People talking about their approach to applying for a job R Job advert & CV L A job interview R Newspaper articles	The passive	Procedures
15 Time p67 Work issues Time management Wasting time	Discussing time in general terms Summarising a talk Discussing time management Making plans using *going to* and *will*	L A talk on time management R A talk on time management R Article: *Life without time* L Conversations: making plans R Web page: *Wasting time*	*Going to* *Going to* vs *will*	Working conditions
16 Getting things done p73 Conversation skills Asking favours Saying 'no' tactfully Being polite	Asking favours using prompts Saying 'no' tactfully Putting a dialogue in order Identifying polite language and using it to re-enact a conversation	L Conversations: asking favours L Conversation: saying 'no' L Conversation: a request, persuasion & a threat L Conversations: asking for an upgrade & complaining about a room		
17 Office gossip p76 Work issues Gossip in the workplace	Using reported speech Reporting gossip Classifying e-mails Interviewing & writing a report	L Conversation: an office rumour L Conversations: office gossip R Newspaper article: *City Council gags workers* R Extracts from e-mails L Interview: changing relations in the workplace	Reported speech	Relationships at work
18 E-commerce p81 Connecting Internet marketing Online shopping Predictions	Completing notes on a discussion Completing a report Emphasising using *... is one thing, but ... is another* Focus group roleplay: marketing to the over-sixties Making predictions using *will*	L Focus group discussion L Emphasising using *... is one thing, but ... is another* R Magazine article: *Shopping from home*	*Will* for future predictions *I think + will*	Shopping & the Internet
19 Working from home p87 Work issues Teleworking	Expressing hypothetical situations using conditionals Identifying advantages & disadvantages Performing a roleplay	R News item: *Go home and work* L Interviews: two people who work from home R Magazine article: *Working at home*	Conditionals (future reference)	Teleworking
20 Working lunch p91 Conversation skills Describing food Chatting over lunch	Putting a dialogue in order Describing food Explaining who does what in your company Identifying and discussing cultural differences in business	L Conversation (in four parts): people from different cultures doing business R Extract about business etiquette in Japan		

Company life

1 Selling your company

First salesman: I made some very valuable contacts today.
Second salesman: I didn't get any orders either. *Anon*

1   The words on the left are from a business presentation. Match them to the definitions on the right.

a	website	1	money you spend on rent, equipment, salaries, etc.
b	potential market	2	companies who put money into new businesses
c	average	3	people who you can sell to
d	costs	4	pay someone to do a job
e	investment	5	a group of web pages on the Internet
f	employ	6	publicity you send to people's homes by post
g	direct mail campaign	7	money you need to establish or expand a business
h	venture capitalists	8	the sum of, for example, ten different numbers divided by ten

a	b	c	d	e	f	g	h

elevator pitch: a concise, carefully planned description about your company that your mother could understand in the time it takes to ride up an elevator. A good elevator pitch is less than 60 seconds long.

2   Use the words in 1 to talk about an idea for a new business.

For example: *Millions of people are learning English. The **potential market** for the new electronic dictionary is enormous.*

3   Read this extract from the web page of a venture capitalist.

The elevator pitch

Present your business idea in 60 seconds or less.

We invite you to make your elevator pitch to Jon Day, technology analyst at netinvest.org, the Internet investment boutique.

a   What exactly do you do?
b   What is your previous experience?
c   What is your competitive advantage?
d   What is your future potential/potential market?
e   How successful are you?
f   How much money do you need?

Call **555 875 4476** during The Investment Hour, Saturdays from 6–7 pm

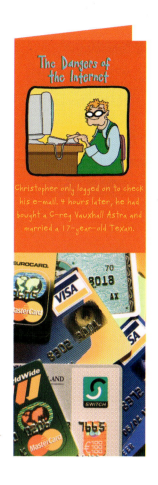

4 Nick Jenkins phoned The Investment Hour with his business idea. Look at the three pictures on this page. What do you think his business is?

5 1.1 Listen to Nick Jenkins' elevator pitch. What are his answers to the questions on the web page in 3?

a _____

b _____

c _____

d _____

e _____

f _____

6 After listening to Nick Jenkins' elevator pitch, Jon Day, the investment analyst, wrote the following report. Complete it using the figures in the box. Then listen again and check your answers.

| 750,000 | £1 billion | 24 | 60% | 92% | 650 | 300,000 |
| £2 million and £3 million | | 50% | £1.20 | £750,000 | 12 | 15,000 |

Moonpig

Moonpig operates a website that allows users to personalise, print and send greetings cards within (a) _____ hours. Users can choose from more than (b) _____ cards and can customise the captions on the cover as well as the greeting.

The founder, Nick Jenkins, has an MBA and previous experience setting up businesses in the former Soviet Union. He employs (c) _____ people at Moonpig.

He says their competitive advantage is that this is one of the few times that you can buy something from the Internet that's actually better than a similar product that you can buy in a shop. They have a (d) _____ digital printing system. Their running costs are low and they make a profit of (e) _____ on each card sold, a margin of (f) _____.

Their potential market is enormous. (g) _____ of the British population buy an average of 12 cards each a year. The greetings card business is worth more than (h) _____ a year in the UK alone and £10 billion worldwide.

At the moment they have (i) _____ users and more and more people are registering each month. Turnover is increasing by (j) _____ a month and they are expecting to be profitable within six months. Their target is to get (k) _____ customers in the UK and (l) _____ worldwide in five years.

They are looking for between (m) _____ of investment to finance marketing in the UK and the US. Their direct mail campaigns are proving very successful, and they are talking to venture capitalists in the US about setting up a website there.

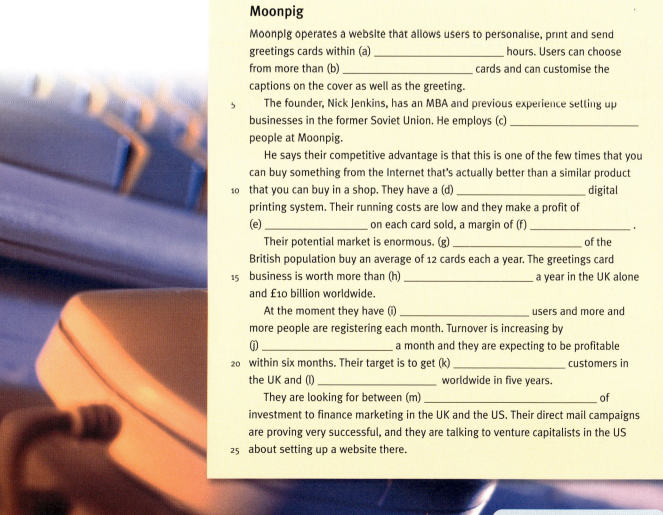

7 What do you think of Nick Jenkins' business idea? Look at page 124 to see what Jon Day, the investment analyst, thought.

> **Grammar link**
>
> for more on the Present Simple and Continuous see page 94

Present Simple vs Present Continuous

8 Complete the chart as in the example. Find two more examples in the report in 6 and add them to the chart.

	Present Simple	Present Continuous	Stable situation	Current situation /activity	Situation of change
92% of the British population buy an average of 12 cards each a year.	✓		✓		
Turnover is increasing by 50% a month.					
He employs 12 people at Moonpig.					
They are looking for between £2 million and £3 million of investment.					

Talking business

Collocations

1 Combine the verbs in A with the words in B. Make as many different combinations as possible. For example: *make a profit*

> A   make   have   hire   run   set up
>
> B   a company   a business   a profit   staff   a website   previous experience

_____   _____
_____   _____
_____   _____
_____   _____
_____   _____

2 Use the collocations in 1 to complete the sentences below. You may need to change the form of the verb.

  a Our investors are happy because we <u>are making a profit</u>.
  b We _____ so that people can get information about our products online.
  c They use a recruiting agency to _____.
  d Giovanni Bianchi _____ which his family owns in Milan.
  e He has the right qualifications for the job but _____ he _____?

3 Choose three collocations from 1 and make your own examples.

Word building

4 The words in brackets are from the report on page 5. They are all important business words. Use the correct form of each to complete the sentences.

Lexis link

for more on the vocabulary of business and the Internet see page 95

a His new business is a great _____. (successful)
b We have good ideas, but we need to convince our _____. (investment)
c As the market grows, they are increasing _____. (product)
d It's a very _____ business. (profit)
e Every day I read the _____ newspapers. (finance)
f We are looking for _____ to start up a new business. (capitalist)

The company web page

1 You are surfing the Internet and you see the web page below. Find words which mean the same as the following:

a move information to a computer from the Internet (para 1) _____
b take to a specific place (para 1) _____
c growth (para 2) _____
d goods or money that a company owns (para 3) _____
e without competition (para 3) _____
f original (para 4) _____
g running after (para 6) _____
h maintain (para 7) _____

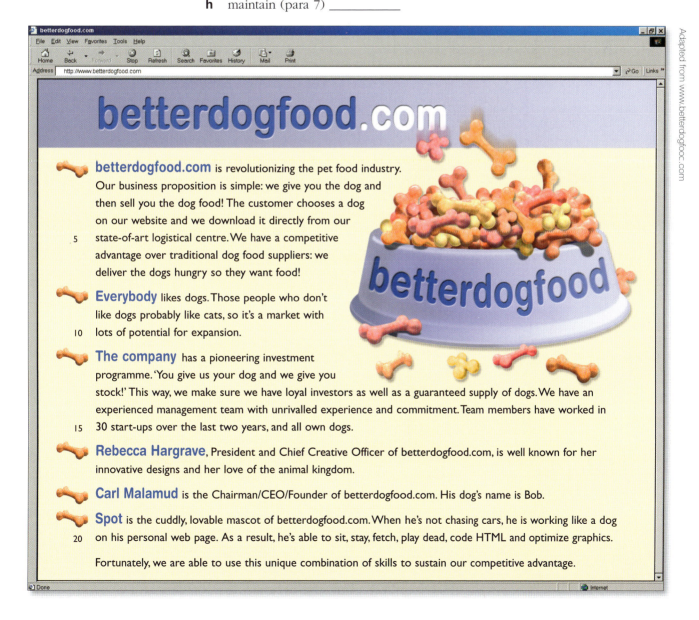

Adapted from www.betterdogfooc.com

betterdogfood.com is revolutionizing the pet food industry. Our business proposition is simple: we give you the dog and then sell you the dog food! The customer chooses a dog on our website and we download it directly from our state-of-art logistical centre. We have a competitive advantage over traditional dog food suppliers: we deliver the dogs hungry so they want food!

Everybody likes dogs. Those people who don't like dogs probably like cats, so it's a market with lots of potential for expansion.

The company has a pioneering investment programme. 'You give us your dog and we give you stock!' This way, we make sure we have loyal investors as well as a guaranteed supply of dogs. We have an experienced management team with unrivalled experience and commitment. Team members have worked in 30 start-ups over the last two years, and all own dogs.

Rebecca Hargrave, President and Chief Creative Officer of betterdogfood.com, is well known for her innovative designs and her love of the animal kingdom.

Carl Malamud is the Chairman/CEO/Founder of betterdogfood.com. His dog's name is Bob.

Spot is the cuddly, lovable mascot of betterdogfood.com. When he's not chasing cars, he is working like a dog on his personal web page. As a result, he's able to sit, stay, fetch, play dead, code HTML and optimize graphics. Fortunately, we are able to use this unique combination of skills to sustain our competitive advantage.

1 Selling your company

2 Reorganise the words to form questions.

a company's the what's name
What's the company's name?

b exactly they do what do
_____

c of competition what is kind there
_____

d their advantage what competitive is
_____

e their is market what potential
_____

f for do they investment how the business get
_____

g behind people company the who are the
_____

h experience previous they what do have
_____

3 Answer the questions in 2 with information about betterdogfood.com.

a _____
b _____
c _____
d _____
e _____
f _____
g _____
h _____
_____
_____

"Whatever you're selling, they're buying."

1 Selling your company

Your dot.com start-up

Fluency 1 Work with a partner. Discuss your ideas for your own dot.com. It can be either serious or humorous. Complete the 'Your dot.com start-up' column in the table below. Then change partner and pitch your idea to your new partner. Listen to your new partner's pitch and take notes.

	Your dot.com start-up	**Your new partner's dot.com start-up**
Name of company		
Product or service		
Potential market		
How you make money		
Management team		
Competition		
Competitive advantage		
Investment needed		

2 Use the framework below to write a web page describing your new partner's company.

_____ (*name of company*)

is a _____ (*type of company*)

The main activity of the company is _____

Their potential market is _____
_____

It makes money by _____

The management team _____
_____

The competition _____
_____

Their competitive advantage is _____
_____
_____

They are looking for investment to _____
_____
_____

Company life  # 2 Women in business

> Women now represent 50% of university graduates. To get the best brains, it's obvious to me that we need more women. *Eivind Reiten, CEO of Norske Hydro*

Fortune 500 = the 500 biggest companies in the USA

Board of Directors = the group of individuals responsible for the running of the entire company

CEO = Chief Executive Officer, the highest level director in the company

1 Complete the statistics using the numbers in the box. Compare your answers with a partner.

4.1%   12.5%   46.5%   two   11.7%

a _____ of all workers in the USA are women.
b _____ of senior managers in the Fortune 500 are women.
c Women represent _____ of top earners.
d Women comprise _____ of individuals serving on Boards of Directors.
e However, there are only _____ women CEOs in the Fortune 500.

Discussion

2 Look at page 124 to check the statistics in 1. Then discuss the questions.
a Is the situation similar in your country?
b Do you think this situation will change in the future?

3 Careers&women.com is a website aimed at women who work in – or would like to work in – technology-related jobs. Read the extract from their site and answer the questions on page 11.

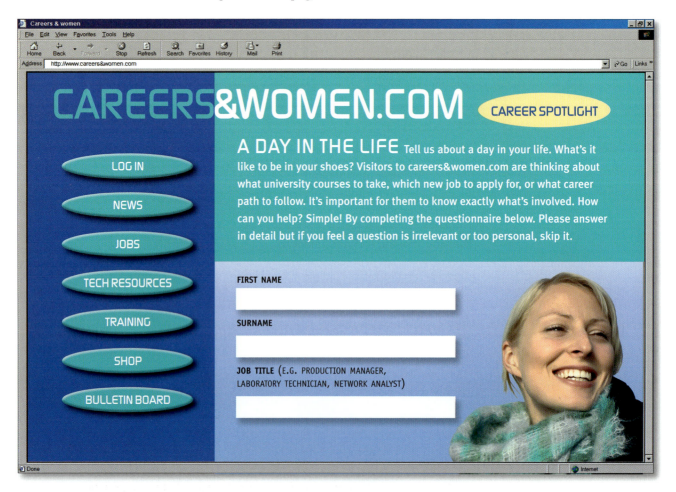

a Who is the questionnaire for? _____

b Why does Careers&women.com want this information? _____

c Do women who respond have to answer all the questions? _____

4 Read the replies of one woman who answered the questions. Match the questions below to her answers.

- How much holiday do you get?
- What sort of company do you work for?
- What do you enjoy most about your work?
- What does your job involve?
- What do you do?
- Have you got any advice for women that are interested in going into your field?
- How much travel does your job involve?
- How many hours a week do you work?
- Do you work late or at the weekend?
- What is the female to male ratio in your position/field?

a _____

In my company they call me a Regional Marketing Manager, that's my job title.

b _____

We're a multinational with offices in 15 different countries around the world.

c _____

I'm in charge of sales support for my country, and I'm also involved in developing new marketing strategies.

d _____

35 hours. I'm based in France and officially that's the maximum number of hours you can work.

e _____

No, I never work later than six. We have a couple of hours off for lunch as well. I usually have a sandwich at my desk, though, and then I like to go for a walk to clear my head.

f _____

Quite a lot. It's mainly within France and occasionally other European countries. Once or twice a year I go back to the States for a meeting at our central office.

g _____

In France we get five weeks a year. It's quite generous compared to the USA.

h _____

I'd say that marketing departments usually have more women than men. At least, that's usually the case in the USA and France, which are the countries I've worked in.

i _____

I love my independence. It's hard work but usually very interesting.

j _____

Get some work experience while you're a student, even if you have to do it for free. Companies are more interested in experience than qualifications. Obviously, you need a degree if you want to be something like an engineer, but it's easier to find a job if you've got some practical experience.

5   **2.1** Two friends are looking at the Careers&women.com website. They are discussing how a woman called Joanne answered the questionnaire. Listen and make notes about how she answered the questions in 4.

6   Complete the conversation between the two friends in 5 with suitable questions. Then listen again and compare your questions with what the speaker says.

   A   Oh, look, here's something in our field.
   B   _____
   A   Design Team Co-ordinator.
   B   Yes, but _____
   A   They produce computer games software.
   B   So, _____
   A   Well, her name's Joanne, and she says that she's responsible for anything design-related in the company. And that it's very rewarding.
   B   What does she most enjoy about the work?
   A   She has a huge amount of responsibility, opportunities to learn, and it never gets boring because the job is always changing.
   B   _____
   A   Up to sixty hours a week.
   B   Sixty hours a week!
   A   Yes, eleven hours on weekdays and a half-day over the weekend.
   B   That's sounds an awful lot.
   A   Yes, but hang on. That's only during development stages. It's usually forty to forty-five hours.
   B   _____
   A   It doesn't say. She doesn't start that early, though. Most days she gets in at around nine thirty, it says.
   B   _____
   A   Let's see. Three out of the fourteen in her company are women, which she says is unusually balanced for the computer games industry.
   B   Balanced! Why?
   A   Because on the whole these companies only employ women as decoration for their stands at conferences.
   B   Well, that doesn't sound very positive. _____
   A   None at all. She never travels because she can do everything from the office. Travelling is for holidays.
   B   And _____
   A   Five weeks a year. Sounds quite generous.
   B   Yes, it's more than most companies offer.
   A   Hmm. It's just the kind of job I'm looking for. I wonder how she got into it.
   B   Be assertive without being rude and stick up for yourself when you're right. That's her advice.

Fluency

7   Work with a partner. Speaker A look at the chart on page 126. Speaker B look at the chart on page 130. Ask questions as in 6 to complete the charts.

8   Ask your partner similar questions and write down the answers.

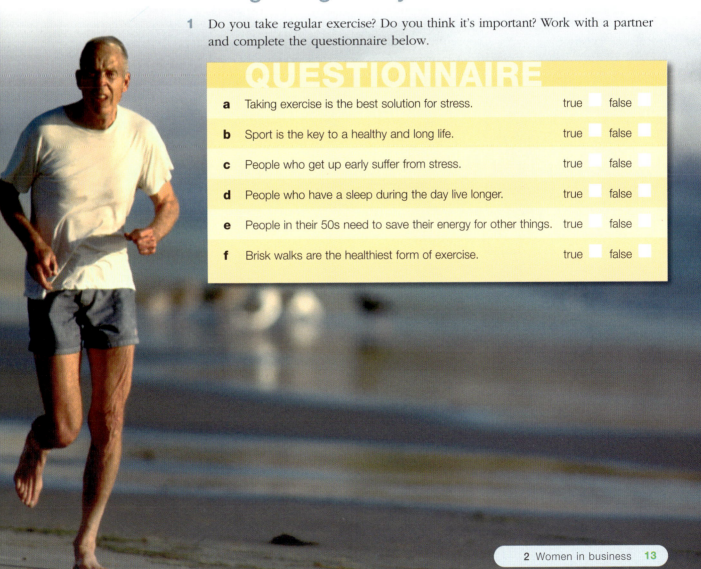

How often do you ...?

Expressing frequency

1 Add a frequency expression to each sentence so that it is true for you.

> always   usually   sometimes   often   every day   every week
> twice a year   once a month   not often   hardly ever   never

Grammar link

for more on expressing frequency see page 96

a I go to work by car.
b I get home late.
c I work at the weekend.
d I have a holiday.
e I feel bored with my job.
f My boss gives me a hard time.
g My computer crashes.
h I find time to relax and enjoy myself.
i I have arguments with people at work.
j I read the financial papers.

2 Complete the 'Action' and 'You' columns in the chart below. Then ask questions to complete the 'Your partner' column.

	Action	You	Your partner
	eat out	once a week	
How often do you ...?			
Do you ... much?			
Do you ever ...?			

Taking things easy

1 Do you take regular exercise? Do you think it's important? Work with a partner and complete the questionnaire below.

QUESTIONNAIRE

a Taking exercise is the best solution for stress.   true ☐ false ☐

b Sport is the key to a healthy and long life.   true ☐ false ☐

c People who get up early suffer from stress.   true ☐ false ☐

d People who have a sleep during the day live longer.   true ☐ false ☐

e People in their 50s need to save their energy for other things.   true ☐ false ☐

f Brisk walks are the healthiest form of exercise.   true ☐ false ☐

2 Women in business   13

2 Now read the article to see if you are correct.

> They say that a healthy body is a healthy mind, but according to a German expert it is lazy people who lead longer and healthier lives. Professor Peter Axt recommends avoiding strenuous activity like aerobics or working out in a gym. 'People who prefer to laze in a hammock instead of running a marathon or who
> 5 take a midday nap instead of playing squash have a better chance of living into old age,' says this scientist. They are also less likely to suffer from professional stress.
>
> He cowrote *On the Joy of Laziness* with his daughter, who is also a doctor. In the book he advises people to 'waste half your time. Just enjoy lazing
> 10 around.' Those who get up early in the morning usually feel stressed for the rest of the day, so his advice is to take it easy.
>
> However, Professor Axt stresses that laziness in only one of the keys to a longer life. In fact, the subtitle of his book is *How best to use your energies*. He argues that if you are too fat, you need more energy to maintain body functions,
> 15 and is in favour of moderate exercise like 'meditative' jogging or brisk walks to 'relax body and spirit at the same time'.
>
> On the other hand, any exertion is not recommended, especially for middle-aged people who should be particularly careful about doing too much sport. Professor Axt believes we have only a limited amount of energy, and people who
> 20 use up their supply more quickly live shorter lives. 'Research shows that people who run long distances into their 50s are using up energy they need for other purposes.'

Lexis link

for more on the vocabulary of work and routines see page 97

3 Underline three expressions which mean 'to relax' or 'to rest'.

4 Choose the best title for the article.
  a ALL WORK AND NO PLAY MAKES JACK A DULL BOY
  b HEALTH RISKS FOR THE OVER 50s
  c SIESTA OR MARATHON?
  d _____ (*your own idea*)

Discussion

5 Discuss the following questions with other people in the class.
  a Do you agree with Professor Axt?
  b What do you do to relax?
  c Do you find it easy to relax?
  d Do you do more or less exercise than **1** you would like to? **2** you think is good for you? Why?

14 2 Women in business

Connecting

3 Telephone talk

> No, I don't know his telephone number. But it was up in the high numbers.
> *John Maynard Keynes, British economist*

Numbers

1   How do you say the following in English?

25%	632,233	$2,000,000	£4.3 m	6.25	5.6234
£3,022	6,576,358	2 + 2 = 4	8 − 2 = 6	5 x 3 = 15	12 ÷ 3 = 4

🔊 **3.1** Now listen and check your answers.

2   Write down eight different figures or calculations. Dictate them to your partner.

3   You are going to read an article about using the telephone in business. Before you read, guess the answers to the following questions. Then read the article to see if you are correct.

  a   In a survey, companies failed to answer _____ of calls within ten rings.
  1 10%   **2** 20%   **3** 50%

  b   _____ of all sales enquiries begin on the telephone.
  1 50%   **2** 70%   **3** 90%

  c   A telephonist could answer _____ calls in a year.
  1 30,000   **2** 300,000   **3** 3,000,000

RINGING IN THE MILLIONS

COMPANIES lose millions of dollars of business through bad telephone handling. A survey found that company switchboards failed to answer one out of five calls within ten rings, or reply to 10% of calls within 20 rings. Ninety percent of all sales enquiries begin on the telephone, so this is the opportunity to project a healthy company image – one of friendliness, efficiency and professionalism. Staff should be aware that bad telephone behaviour can result in millions of
10 dollars in lost revenue. In the insurance business, for example, failure to answer promptly could see a policy of a quarter of a million dollars go straight to the competition!

   A single telephone receptionist can answer as many as 300,000 calls a year. Companies should train personnel in the skills of transferring a call,
15 placing calls on hold, dealing with angry callers, answering correspondence by phone, using a caller's name, and taking messages correctly. Callers should not hear expressions like 'she's just gone out' or 'he's not with us anymore'. Surveys show that customers want a prompt response by a real person (not a machine) who can make a decision.

20   For a great many of a firm's customers, the first – and often the only – impression they carry in their minds is the one generated by the people they talk to on the phone. The quality of a firm's response to a call is one of the chief factors in creating a perception of good or bad service. And remember, more business is lost through poor service than by poor product performance.

Adapted from Ringing up the Millions by Brendan Walsh

4 The following figures appear in the article on page 15. Can you remember what they refer to?

   a one out of five _____

   b millions of dollars _____

   c a quarter of a million dollars _____

   d first _____

Discussion

5 Discuss the following questions with a partner.

   a Does your company have any policies on phone use? Does it provide training?
   b What functions does your phone have? Do you know how to use them all?
   c Do you prefer to use a mobile or a landline?

6 'More business is lost through bad service than by poor product performance.' Do you agree?

Telephone skills

7 Match the six telephone skills listed in paragraph 2 of *Ringing in the millions* to the following examples of telephone language.

   a A Can I have extension 305, please?
       B I'm afraid the line is engaged. Will you hold?

   placing calls on hold

   b A Could I just check that? You need 50 units by Friday, and Mr Johansson can contact you on 943 694726.
       B Yes, that's correct.
       A Right, Mr Smith. I'll give him the message as soon as he's free.

   _____

   c A ... and it really isn't good enough.
       B Yes, Mr Wright. I understand what you're saying and I do apologise for the error. As soon as Mr Downs is back I'll ask him to get in contact with you. I'm really sorry about this.
       A Right, thank you. I realise it's not your fault.

   _____

   d A Could I have the Sales Department, please?
       B One moment, please. Just putting you through now.

   _____

   e A Shonagh Clark speaking.
       B Hello, I'm phoning you about your letter of 12th June.

   _____

   f A This is Jorgen Bode here. Could I speak to Jean Simmons, please?
       B Oh, I'm sorry, Mr Bode, but Ms Simmons isn't in the office right now. Can I ask her to call you back? Or I can contact her on her mobile if it's urgent.

   _____

3 Telephone talk

Customer frustration

1. Complete the list of telephone frustrations using the verbs in the box. Then put ticks in the columns according to your level of frustration for each one.

> get   play   put   get   listen   return   take   get   transfer   repeat   call   get

QUESTIONNAIRE

		NOT PLEASED	UNHAPPY	HOPPING MAD
a	They _____ irritating music when you're put on hold.	☐	☐	☐
b	You _____ cut off in the middle of your call.	☐	☐	☐
c	People you call _____ a long time to answer.	☐	☐	☐
d	They _____ you on hold and forget about you.	☐	☐	☐
e	You _____ an answer phone.	☐	☐	☐
f	They _____ you to another person and you have to _____ your enquiry.	☐	☐	☐
g	They don't _____ properly to what you are saying.	☐	☐	☐
h	You continually _____ an engaged tone when you _____ someone.	☐	☐	☐
i	People don't _____ your calls.	☐	☐	☐
j	You _____ through to a voicemail system.	☐	☐	☐

2. Look on page 124 to see what the five most frustrating problems are according to Brendan Walsh.

3 Telephone talk

Could you tell me ...?

Indirect questions

1 🔊 3.2 You use indirect questions to sound more polite. Complete the dialogue below. Then listen to see if you are correct.

A InterAir, can I help you?
B Yes, please. I'd like some information about a flight arriving from Munich.
A Yes. Do you _____
B The flight number? I'm not sure. I know it leaves Munich at 1730.
A Oh, yes, that's IA 345.
B Yes, that's it. Could _____ gets in?
A Yes, the arrival time is 1910.
B 1910. Do you _____ any delay?
A No, the flight is on time.
B Right, thank you very much.
A You're welcome. Goodbye.

2 Look at the prompts on page 124 and practise the conversation with a partner.

3 Look at the chart below. Then rephrase the questions using *Do you know ...?* or *Could you tell me ...?*

Do you know ... Could you tell me ...	how long it takes? where the airport is?
	if she got my message? if you'll finish the order on time?

> **Grammar link**
> for more on indirect questions see page 98

a What time does the flight leave?
   _____

b Which terminal does it leave from?
   _____

c How far is the factory from the airport?
   _____

d Which car hire company is it?
   _____

e Which models do they have available?
   _____

f Do I need an international driving licence?
   _____

g Where are we staying?
   _____

h Is it a nice place?
   _____

i Have they booked a meeting room?
   _____

4   Work with a partner. Speaker B see page 132.

Speaker A You are travelling on business in the UK. When you finish there you are going straight to the USA for a special sales conference. You expected to receive information about this trip from your office, but the datalink in your hotel doesn't work, and you don't have access to your e-mail account. Ring your office to get the necessary information. Ask the questions in 3. Make a note of all the information.

Telephone phrases

Match the following to make telephone expressions.

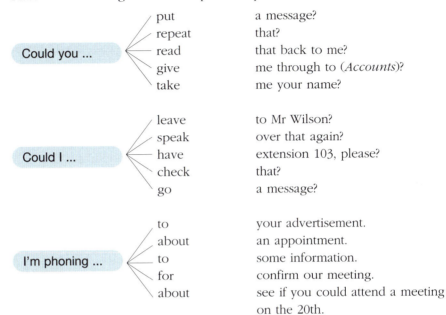

Could you ...	put	a message?
	repeat	that?
	read	that back to me?
	give	me through to (Accounts)?
	take	me your name?

Could I ...	leave	to Mr Wilson?
	speak	over that again?
	have	extension 103, please?
	check	that?
	go	a message?

I'm phoning ...	to	your advertisement.
	about	an appointment.
	to	some information.
	for	confirm our meeting.
	about	see if you could attend a meeting on the 20th.

Lexis link

for more on telephone vocabulary see page 98

Sales contacts

1   **3.3** The sales team at *ADH Graphics* uses the form below to record the details of all phone calls with potential clients. Listen to the conversation and complete the form.

Phone Contact Form ADH Graphics

Date: Wednesday 14th May
Call initiated by: Client
Call handler: B. White

Client: Bellstone & Smith

Address: (a) _____, Clapham Rd, London SW14

Contact: Mr Clarkson

Position: (b) Head of _____

Tel: (c) _____

E-mail: clarkson.bellstone@lineone.com

Nature of business: Elevator manufacturer

Purpose of call:
Wants estimate for printing a (d) _____ of (e) _____ pages. Copies: (f) _____.
Estimates also for (g) _____ and (h) _____ copies. Size: (i) _____ in black & white. Cover in colour. Will supply material on disk or CD.

Comments:
They are updating all their manuals, so could give us more work if the price is right.

Action required: Visit client with (j) _____
By whom: B. White
Date and time: (k) _____ _____ May at 10 am

Roleplay 2   Work with a partner and practise telephoning for information and taking notes. Speaker A see page 126. Speaker B see page 130.

Conversation skills

4 Networking

A gossip talks about others, a bore talks about himself – and a brilliant conversationalist talks about you. Anon

1 **4.1** Rick Van Looy and Florent Rondele meet in a hotel bar after dinner. Listen to **Conversation 1** and answer the questions.

a What does Florent do? _____
b What does Rick do? _____
c Do they know each other? _____

Now listen to **Conversation 2** and answer the questions.

a Where are the speakers? _____
b One of the speakers asks 'Does this belong to you?' What do you think 'this' is? _____
c Where are the speakers going? _____
d Why? _____

2 Listen again and complete the questions that are asked in the conversations.

	Question word	Auxiliary	Subject	Verb	etc.
a		Do	you	mind	if I join you?
b		Are	you		from around here, then?
c	What	_____	_____	do?	
d		_____	you	_____	sports equipment?
e	How many stores	_____	_____	got?	
f	What line of business	_____	_____		in?
g		Do	_____	_____	it?
h		Are	you	_____	a store here, then?
i		_____	you	_____	something to drink?
j		Does	_____	belong	_____ _____ ?
k		_____	you	_____	the time?
l		Do	_____	_____	soon?
m		Do	_____	_____	Bangkok?
n		_____	this		your first trip there?

3 How are questions b, f, and n in 2 different to the others?

_____
_____

20 4 Networking

4 Write questions for the answers in **bold**.

a <u>Who do you work for?</u>   **IBM**.

b _____

_____ **Berlin**. Our offices are in the city centre.

c _____ **In the Royal**. It's a great hotel.

d _____ **No**, only French.

e _____ He's talking **to a client**.

f _____

_____ I'm an **accountant**.

g _____ **Yes**, two boys aged seven and ten.

h _____ **Portugal**. I was born in Lisbon.

i _____ **Yes**, I am – in fact, this is my wife, Yuki.

j _____ **No**, I don't. There's no golf course near where I live. I play squash.

k _____

_____ **Yes**. I met her last year at a conference in Vienna.

Answers on page 124

5 Your company has sent you to an international meeting. It starts in five minutes. You don't know the person sitting next to you. Use the chart below to make conversation and to find out about them.

Question word	Auxiliary	Subject	Verb	etc.
			live	
			work	here
Where	do		do	English
What	does	you	doing	at the moment
How	are	your company	have	any other languages
Why	has	he	got	your job
When	do	she	like	this book
How many employees	are	they	go	any children
	have		travel	to work
			studying	much in your work
			speak	

Talking about other people

1 4.2 Look at the conversation below. Number the lines in the correct order. Then listen and check your answers.

☐ What's he like?

☐ Yes, isn't he Director of Business Development at Guinness?

[1] Do you know Jan Nowacki?

☐ The National Bank of Poland, that's interesting. Do you have any contact with him in your work?

☐ Not any longer. Now he's the Public Relations Manager at the National Bank of Poland.

☐ He's a nice chap. You'd like him.

☐ Not really, but I occasionally play golf with him.

2 Which parts of the conversation could you replace with the expressions below?

 a Have you ever met Do you know
 b doesn't he work for _____
 c bump into him at conferences _____
 d I don't like him much really. _____
 e I don't anymore. _____
 f What do you think of him? _____
 g You'd get on well. _____

3 Look at the business cards below which show the jobs five people did before and what they do now. (One of them is retired). Work with a partner. Using the conversation in 1 as a model, have conversations about the people on the cards. Add comments about their personalities and talents using the phrases in the box.

> He/She's an interesting person.   He/She's rather reserved.
> He/She's a good laugh.   He/She's a bit arrogant.
> He/She's a bit of a bore.   He/She always has the latest gossip.

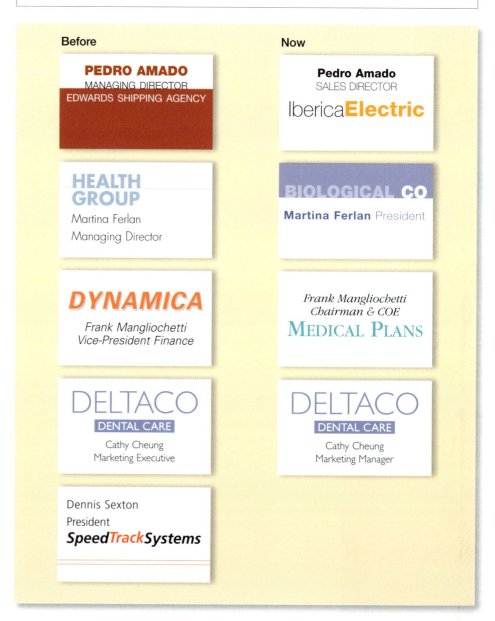

4 Now think about some people you know and have similar conversations about them.

5 Company histories

> History is more or less bunk. It's tradition. We don't want tradition. We want to live in the present and the only history that is worth a tinker's damn is the history we make today. *Henry Ford, American car manufacturer*

1 Read the history of Nintendo below. Complete the text using the words and phrases in the box.

> sales of   microprocessor   subsidiary   one billionth game pack
> hand-held game system   more than 500,000   a breakthrough game concept
> manufacturing games   sales records   corporate headquarters
> first playing cards   anniversaries of

NINTENDO Co. Ltd, of Kyoto, Japan, is the worldwide leader in the creation of interactive entertainment. Nintendo manufactures and markets hardware and software for its popular home video game systems, including the Nintendo 64 and GameBoy, the world's best-selling video game system.

1902   Fusajiro Yamauchi, great grandfather of the present president, **manufactures** the _____ in Japan.

1933   Mr Yamauchi **founds** Yamauchi Nintendo & Co.

1963   The company **changes** its name to Nintendo Co. Ltd. and starts _____ in addition to playing cards.

1970   Nintendo **reconstructs** and **enlarges** its _____.

1975   The company **develops** a video game system.

1976   It **uses** a _____ in a video game system for the first time.

1980   Nintendo **establishes** a _____, Nintendo of America Inc.

1985   The company **starts** _____ the Nintendo Entertainment System (NES) in America.

1987   NES **reaches** number one selling toy status in America.

1989   Nintendo **introduces** GameBoy, the first portable _____ with interchangeable game packs.

1995   The company **celebrates** the sale of the _____.

1996   They **launch** Nintendo 64 in Japan on June 23, selling _____ systems the first day.

1998   Nintendo **releases** Pokemon, _____ for GameBoy, which generates a worldwide collecting craze.

1999   The company **expands** the Pokemon franchise.

2001   With the 20th _____ Nintendo characters Mario and Donkey Kong, GameBoy Advanced and the Nintendo Game Cube home video game console hit the market. The US launch of Game Cube on November 18 smashes previous US _____.

Past Simple: regular verbs

2 The fifteen verbs in **bold** in 1 have regular forms in the Past Simple: infinitive + *-ed / -d.*

For example: *start → start**ed**   release → release**d***

The pronunciation of *-ed* can be /d/, /t/, or /ɪd/. Write the Past Simple of the verbs in **bold** in 1 in the table below, according to their pronunciation.

Group 1	Group 2	Group 3
/d/	/t/	/ɪd/
used	released	started
_____	_____	_____
_____	_____	_____
_____	_____	_____
	_____	

Lexis link
for more on business verbs see page 101

3 🔊 **5.1** Listen to someone talking about the history of Nintendo. Check your answers in 2.

4 Write five questions about Nintendo's history. Use the Past Simple.

_____
_____
_____
_____
_____

5 Write five sentences about Nintendo using the Past Simple. They can be true or false. Work with a partner. Close your books and test each other on the history of Nintendo by reading out your sentences and saying if the other person's sentences are true. If they are false, correct them. Who can remember the most?

Who really invented the Internet?

1 🔊 **5.2** You are going to listen to a radio documentary on the history of the Internet. First, do the quiz below. Then listen to see if you are correct.

Leonard Kleinrock, a computer scientist at UCLA, stands next to the refrigerator-sized computer that made the first-ever connection to what was to become the Internet.

QUIZ
The internet

a In which year did Leonard Kleinrock connect the first two computers?
1 1969   **2** 1975   **3** 1983

b What was the first message sent on the Internet?
1 'hello'   **2** 'lo'   **3** 'log in'

c What did the first version of the Internet connect?
1 military installations   **2** government buildings   **3** universities

d In which year was the first international computer connection made?
1 1969   **2** 1973   **3** 1983

e What is the 'universal language' of the Internet?
1 English   **2** Java Script   **3** TCP/IP

f What was the name of the first browser?
1 Netscape   **2** Mosaic   **3** Gopher

5 Company histories

2 Listen again and number the events below in the correct order.

☐ Bob Kahn and Vincent Cerf invent a software for connecting computers on the Internet.
☐ Professor Kleinrock connects two computers.
☐ Ray Tomlinson sends the first e-mail.
☐ The first version of the Internet links four American universities.
☐ Users join the first USENET newsgroups.
☐ The first Internet browser becomes available.
☐ The Advanced Research Projects Agency starts work on ARPANET.
☐ The number of hosts (computers providing Internet services) reaches 30,000,000.
☐ An 'official language' of the Internet is established.

3 Complete the article with the verbs in the box in the Past Simple. Some of them are irregular.

> join link send become increase mark begin crash watch
> establish invent become reach call want

BIRTH OF THE INTERNET

Was the Internet born in 1969 or in 1983? It all depends on who you talk to. In 1965, the Advanced Research Projects Agency under the US Department of Defense (a) _____ work on a system to connect computers. They (b) _____ the project ARPANET.

On September 2nd, 1969, Professor Leonard Kleinrock connected the first two machines. Twenty people (c) _____ in a laboratory at the University of California as meaningless data flowed between two computers along a 15 foot grey cable. For many people, that day (d) _____ the birth of today's Internet.

The next month they sent the first message on the Net to a computer at Stanford University. The message was 'lo'. They (e) _____ to send the words 'log in' but when they typed 'g' the system (f) _____. In fact the first word was quite appropriate, as a phonetic version of 'hello'.

By January 1970 ARPANET (g) _____ computers in four American universities, and by the following year there were 23 hosts in the system, connecting different universities and research institutes.

In 1973 Ray Tomlinson (h) _____ the first e-mail via ARPANET. In the same year it also went international, connecting hosts in England and Norway.

Another landmark was in 1979 when two graduate students at Duke University (i) _____ the first USENET newsgroups. Users from all over the world (j) _____ these discussion groups to talk about the Net, politics, religion and thousands of other subjects.

In 1974 Bob Kahn and Vincent Cerf (k) _____ a software that allowed ARPANET to connect to other networks using different operating systems. The software, called TCP/IP, (l) _____ the universal language of the Internet on January 1st, 1983. Some people say that this was the true birth of the Net.

More and more networks joined the system and the number of hosts (m) _____ dramatically: from 10,000 in 1984 to 100,000 in 1987.

By the early 1990s the World Wide Web was the most popular way of browsing the web, and the network was accessible to anyone in the world with a computer. In 1992 the number of hosts (n) _____ 1,000,000.

In 1993, Mosaic (o) _____ available. This was the first graphics-based browser of the type we all use today. The growth rate of the Internet was an incredible 341% and by 1998 there were over 30,000,000 hosts.

4 Listen again and check your answers.

Asking questions

5   In pairs, ask and answer questions about the history of the Internet using the word prompts.

   a   When / Professor Kleinrock / connect / first two computers?
   _____

   b   Where / send / first message?
   _____

   c   What / Ray Tomlinson / send / 1973?
   _____

   d   Why / users / join / USENET groups?
   _____

   e   When / TCP/IP / become / official language?
   _____

   f   How much / the Internet / grow / 1993?
   _____

6   The questions in 5 use the following structure:

Question word	did	Subject	Infinitive	etc.
When	did	Professor Kleinrock	connect	two computers?

When you do not know the subject, you use the following structure:

	Who/What	Verb in Past Simple	etc.
~~Who did send the first e-mail?~~	Who	sent	the first e-mail?
~~What did happen?~~	What	happened?	

This usually only happens with 'who' and 'what'.

Questions with no subject

7   Look at the chart below and practise asking and answering questions like this. *Who did Sarah fax? Jack. Who phoned Jack? Jane.*

Grammar link
for more on the Past Simple see page 100

8   Write five questions using both structures in 6 about either the history of the Internet or the history of your company.

When was the last time you ...?

9 Use the verbs on the left with the words and phrases on the right to ask your partner questions beginning *When was the last time you ...?* Then ask follow-up questions. For example:

A **When was the last time you** sent an e-mail?
B This morning.
A Who did you send it to?
B To a customer.
A What was it about?

Use the phrases in the box, if you like.

> I never do / have.   I really can't remember.   It was a long time ago.
> I'm not sure.

Speaker A	
send	an interview
find	a phone call
travel	an e-mail
make	on business
take	something useful on the Internet
go	on a course
eat	on business
have	a taxi

Speaker B	
take	a car
download	late for a meeting
deal	a plane
negotiate	to a useful meeting
go	a new tie
buy	a virus
hire	with a complaint
arrive	a deal

Company history

Fluency

Write a web page giving the history of a company you know about or one you have invented. You may find some of the words in the box useful.

> found   establish   begin   manufacture   develop   achieve   reach   launch
> expand   produce   want   increase

Include information about the following:

- the origins of the company, who founded it and when
- key dates in its history
- the opening of new offices or factories
- important orders or contracts it obtained
- periods of important growth
- introduction of new products or services
- establishment of subsidiaries
- appointment of key personalities in its management
- significant recent events

"Well, that's just uncanny! How did you know that we formed the company in the early '70s?"

Connecting

6 Correspondence

> Unless one is a genius, it is best to aim at being intelligible.
> *Anthony Hope (Sir Anthony Hope Hawkins), British novelist*

1 Read the following article from a business magazine and discuss the questions with a partner.

Does grammar matter?

According to a report published recently, standards in written English are falling. This is mainly because people see the e-mail as an informal way of communicating where the normal rules of grammar and punctuation do not apply. In a survey by MSN, two-thirds of those aged 18–24 admitted that they were more concerned
5   about the content than the grammatical correctness of their e-mails. One in four of older users also said they were not concerned about grammatical correctness in their messages.

Surprisingly, in the same survey, most people said they were annoyed by errors in the e-mails they
10 received. This intolerance is even greater when it comes to conventional letters. In another survey by the UK's Royal Mail, bosses said they would not do business with companies whose correspondence had mistakes in it. Unbelievably,
15 they thought it was worse than over charging. The survey calculated that bad writing skills could be costing offending firms £2bn in lost contracts.

a Do you see e-mails as an informal way of communicating?

b If someone sends you a badly written e-mail, do you find it annoying? Are you more tolerant if you know they are not writing in their first language?

c Do you think the bosses in the survey were right? Why/why not?

Discussion 2 Answer the questions. Then discuss your results with people in the class.

QUESTIONNAIRE

How often do you ...	every hour	every day	every week	not often	other
a use the telephone?	☐	☐	☐	☐	☐
b send and receive faxes?	☐	☐	☐	☐	☐
c look at your e-mail?	☐	☐	☐	☐	☐
d send things by courier?	☐	☐	☐	☐	☐
e use internal mail?	☐	☐	☐	☐	☐
f use the postal service?	☐	☐	☐	☐	☐
g have face to face meetings?	☐	☐	☐	☐	☐

3   What are the advantages and disadvantages of the different methods of communication in 2? Think about the following:

> bulk and weight   signatures   reliability   confidentiality   convenience
> training   technology   image   handwriting   artwork and photographs
> cost   speed   quality

4   Write a summary of your conclusions in 2 and 3. For example:

All of us use internal mail about twice a week. It's reliable, cheaper than the postal service and you can send packages of all sizes. Some people use fax to send documents which need a signature.

On-the-spot decisions

1   **6.1** Listen to the telephone conversation between Cathy Slater, the caller, and Jim Kutz, who answers the call. Answer the questions.

   a   Who does Cathy want to speak to? _____
   b   Why? _____
   c   Why did she send him a fax? _____
   d   What solution does Jim offer? _____
   _____
   e   What is Jim's e-mail address? _____

Taking decisions

2   Some situations require on-the-spot decisions. What did the speakers in 1 say? Circle the correct answers.

I'll send you / **I'm going to send** / **I'm sending**	a copy of the certificate.
Don't worry,	**I'll deal** / **I'm going to deal** / **I'm dealing** with the e-mail straight away.

You use *will* + infinitive to show that you are making an on-the-spot decision and to promise action.

3   Complete the conversation below using *will* + infinitive.

   A   Have we got a decision from Jim about the Mason contract?
   B   No, don't worry, I _____
   A   I tried – there's no answer.
   B   Well, I _____
   A   You can't – our intranet is down.
   B   Never mind – I _____
   A   I don't think we have their fax number.
   B   Well, in that case, I _____
   A   Oh, come on, that'll take far too long.
   B   So, we _____
   A   Oh, that's a bit expensive.

4   **6.2** Listen and compare your answer to 3.

Grammar link

for more on *will* for unplanned decisions see page 102

5 Work with a partner. Speaker A look at the chart below. Speaker B look at the chart on page 132.

Speaker A Choose a problem from the table and tell Speaker B. Begin *I've got a problem ...* Speaker B will offer a solution and then tell you about a problem. React using one of the solutions below. Say *Don't worry, I'll ...*

For example:
A I've got a problem, the battery in my mobile's flat.
B Don't worry, I'll lend you mine.

Problems	Solutions
I've got a headache.	... take you to the airport.
We didn't get your fax.	... fax the details to you instead.
This report has lots of errors in it.	... show you how it works.
I can't remember his phone number.	... explain them to you.
I haven't booked my flight to Berlin.	... call the IT technician.
I need three copies of this proposal.	... phone you this afternoon.
I don't know anything about this company.	... change the ink cartridge.

Answers on page 131

An important order

1 **6.3** Look at the fax below. It confirms the details of an order made on the telephone. Listen to the conversation and complete the missing information.

FAX
STERNHydraulics

Limmatstrasse 450
8030 ZÜRICH
Tel. 01 360 4464

Dear John,

Further to our phone conversation today, I would like to confirm the following order:

Hydraulic pump ref: (a)_____

Number of units: (b)_____

To be delivered no later than (c)_____.

Please let us know of any problems in processing this order. We are especially concerned about receiving the parts on time as it is for a (d)_____ customer.

Best regards,

Elena Moretti

Stern Hydraulics

2. Work with a partner. Practise the conversation using the prompts.

A S-A-G / help?
B Yes / speak / John Bird?
A afraid / not / office / now / can / message?
B Oh, dear! / urgent order / we / five hydraulic pumps / June 22nd
A Just / minute / tell / name please?
B sorry / Elena Moretti / Stern Hydraulics / Switzerland
A Right / take down / details / get John / contact / say five units?
B Yes / reference / SG 94321
A SG 94321 / five units
B yes / right / important thing / delivery date / June 22nd
A not think / a problem
B good / for / new customer
A I see / when John comes / tell him immediately / confirm / order / writing?
B yes / course / thanks / much
A you / welcome / goodbye
B goodbye

3. Later that day John Bird phoned back. Work with a partner. Try to complete the conversation using the words and phrases in the box.

| is that | more business | help you | could I speak to | in touch |
| phoning | it's quite | good | all the details | worry | worried |

John _____ Elena Moretti, please?

Elena Speaking. _____ John?

John Yes. Hello, Elena. I'm _____ back about your order.

Elena Yes, _____ urgent.

John Don't _____. I've got _____ in your fax. No problem.

Elena That's _____. I was _____ about it.

John Well, can I _____ with anything else?

Elena No, but I hope we get _____ from this customer.

John Yes, of course. Okay, I'll be _____. Bye for now.

Elena Goodbye.

4. 6.4 Now listen to the conversation in 3 to see if you are correct.

5. Later, Elena received this confirmation of her order. What is the mistake?

SAG CONFIRMATION OF ORDER DH010601 June 1st
Order received: May 23rd
Part Ref. Number: SG 94321
No. of units: 5
Delivery required: July 7th
Processed by:
John Bird

6 Correspondence

6   6.5 Elena phoned SAG to tell John Bird about the mistake. Number the lines of the conversation in the correct order. Then listen and check.

☐ S-A-G, can I help you?

☐ No, it's not your fault. Just ask John to phone me.

☐ Right, Elena, leave it with me. I'm terribly sorry about this.

☐ Oh, hello, Elena. I'm afraid John isn't here at the moment. Can I take a message?

☐ Yes, it says July 7th, but the agreed delivery date was June 22nd. It's really important.

☐ Yes, this is Elena Moretti from Stern Hydraulics. Could I speak to John Bird, please?

☐ Oh, dear. Can you give me the details?

☐ All right, then. Bye for now.

☐ Thank you. I'm not at all happy about this. A lot depends on this order.

☐ I see. Well, I'll tell him as soon as he comes in.

☐ Yes, he sent me an order confirmation – the reference is DH010601 – but the delivery date is wrong.

☐ Goodbye.

Answers on page 125

Fluency

7   When John Bird got back to the office, he tried to phone Elena but couldn't get through. He decided to send an e-mail. Write his e-mail using the prompts below.

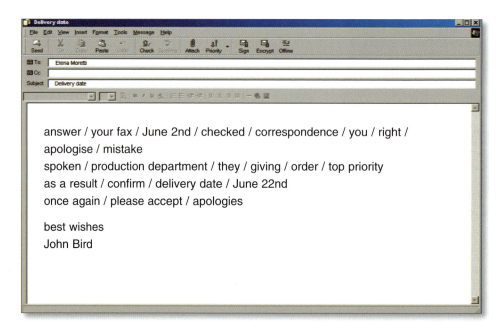

answer / your fax / June 2nd / checked / correspondence / you / right / apologise / mistake
spoken / production department / they / giving / order / top priority
as a result / confirm / delivery date / June 22nd
once again / please accept / apologies

best wishes
John Bird

Lexis link

for more on the vocabulary of business communication see page 102

Fluency

8   On June 22nd the parts didn't arrive. They didn't arrive until June 30th. Elena phoned John again. Work with a partner and act out the conversation. Speaker A see below. Speaker B see page 132.

Speaker A
You are Elena Moretti. You are furious with John Bird. The order arrived late and as a result you will get no more orders from your customer. SAG let you down and you think John Bird is responsible. You are also angry about the fact that he never returns your calls and always makes mistakes. Unless he offers you some compensation (such as heavy discounts on future orders), tell him you will take your business elsewhere.

7 Making comparisons

Shall I compare thee to a summer's day? *William Shakespeare, Sonnet 18, III:5, 1599*

1. What features do you expect a good hotel to provide? Tick the features you expect. Add your own ideas to the list.

   ☐ widescreen television   ☐ historic architecture   ☐ swimming pool
   ☐ high-speed Internet connections   ☐ beautiful surroundings   ☐ fitness rooms
   ☐ convenient location   ☐ sauna
   ☐ 24-hour room service

2. 🔊 **7.1** It's two o'clock in the afternoon. A guest arrives at a hotel and checks in. Listen to the conversation and answer the questions.

   a What does the receptionist offer the guest? Why? _____

   b What does the guest need to do? _____

3. Practise the conversation with a partner using the prompts below.

   Receptionist afternoon
   Guest afternoon / reservation / name of
   Receptionist yes / right / have / flight?
   Guest yes / too bad / bit long
   Receptionist see / passport?
   Guest course / here
   Receptionist thank / room / 301 / like / breakfast sent / room?
   Guest breakfast? / yes / nice
   Receptionist tea or coffee?
   Guest coffee please / need / send / e-mail
   Receptionist no problem / find / terminal / room
   Guest right / thanks
   Receptionist welcome / good stay

Global hotels

1. Before you read the article on page 34, decide if the following statements are true or false. Then read to see if you are correct.

		True	False
a	InterContinental Hotels keep worldwide records on client preferences.	☐	☐
b	Most independent hotels can't afford sufficient staff to provide the services of a multinational hotel chain.	☐	☐
c	Hotels make most of their money from food and drink.	☐	☐
d	American clients are more used to 'brand name' hotel chains.	☐	☐
e	In Europe it is more difficult to build hotels than in the USA.	☐	☐
f	A seventeenth century castle is an ideal site for a multinational chain hotel.	☐	☐

HOTEL CHAIN TAKEOVER

Any place, any time, anywhere, the chances are the bathroom will be on the left of your room.

Travellers get off long-haul flights and receive a carefully prepared welcome at the InterContinental Hotel in Sydney. Receptionists offer refreshments suitable for the time zone which guests have just come from. It is early afternoon in Sydney's high summer, but they greet British businessmen suffering from jetlag with a breakfast of toast, marmalade and cornflakes.

The hotel chain even checks its worldwide database of guests to anticipate which newspaper each customer takes, in order to offer a 'local equivalent'.

The hotel industry is becoming more and more globalised. International chains are encircling the world, taking over local operators. In the US, 75% of hotels have a well-known brand, compared with just 25% in Europe. Size is becoming more important as customer expectations rise. International business travellers want Internet connections, widescreen televisions and push-button blinds in every room. They want faxes delivered to their rooms at all hours of the night and the ability to order *foie gras* at four o'clock in the morning. This means employing more staff than most independent operators can afford.

Between a third and half of hotels' revenue comes from food and drink, but these only contribute 20% to 30% of profit. The real profits come from the rooms, so for most operators the principle objective is to improve occupancy. Loyalty card schemes are becoming increasingly elaborate. They can record guests' preferences for well-cooked steak, ground-floor rooms or feather-free pillows.

However, there are limits to the internationalisation of European hotels. It's much simpler to build hotels in the US than in Europe because there is so much space in the US. If you want a hotel, you can just build it. In Europe there are fewer opportunities for construction, so there are more conversions. Converted buildings aren't as easy to adapt to the US chain model as new buildings because the rooms are different shapes and sizes, so the standard 'template' doesn't work.

It is difficult to turn a seventeenth century castle into a Holiday Inn, so some independent operators still prosper. That is bad news for the ideal guest of a multinational chain. He likes to wake up anywhere in the world in the knowledge that the bathroom is on the left, the blinds are blue and the phone is on the wall, six and a half inches above the bedside table.

Adapted from Hotels play the global brand game by Andrew Clark © The Guardian 2001

2 Find words in the article which mean:
- **a** long distance journey by plane long-haul flight
- **b** area of the world with the same time _____
- **c** tiredness caused by travelling long distances by plane _____
- **d** be able to pay for _____
- **e** income _____
- **f** do well economically _____

3 Complete the sentences with the words in 2.
  a When travellers arrive here from the USA, they often suffer from _____.
  b Most families can _____ two cars.
  c To get here from the UK you have to take a _____.
  d The _____ from tourism is important for the economy.
  e We are in the same _____ as Prague.
  f The agricultural and food processing industries _____ because of the good climate.

4 Are the sentences in 3 true for your country? Change the sentences which are not true.

Comparatives

5 Look at this sentence from the article on page 34.
  *It's much **simpler** to build hotels in the US **than** in Europe.*
  Find five other examples of how things are compared in the article. Underline them.

Road test

1 Compare the two cars below using the information in the table and the adjectives in the box. You may need to use some adjectives more than once.
  *The Maserati is **more expensive than** the Chevrolet.*
  *The Chevrolet has a **longer** guarantee **than** the Maserati.*

| powerful | good | expensive | economical | attractive | fast | long |
| high | wide | heavy | light | big | small | stylish | sexy |

Maserati 3200 GT

Chevrolet Corvette

	Maserati 3200 GT	Chevrolet Corvette
Price	89,401 euros	59,997 euros
Guarantee	2 years	3 years or 100,000 km
Motor	3,217 cc	5,665 cc
Power	370 brake horse power	344 brake horse power
Top speed	280 km/hr	274 km/hr
Consumption	15.07 litres/100kms	13.19 litres/100kms
Length	4.51 m	4.56 m
Width	1.82 m	1.87 m
Height	1.31 m	1.21 m
Size of boot	220 litres	320 litres
Fuel tank	90 litres	70 litres
Weight	1,620 kg	1,455 kg

Answers on page 128

Discussion

2 Work with a partner and discuss the following questions.
  a Do you have a car? What make and model is it? How does it compare to other cars in the same price range? Will you buy the same car again or something different?
  b Have you had other cars in the past? If you have, what were they? How did they compare with the car you have now?
  c Do you have a dream car? What is it?

World leaders

Superlatives

1. Speaker A look at the instructions below. Speaker B look at the instructions on page 131.

   Speaker A
   Look at the tables below. Your partner has the missing information. Ask questions to complete the tables. For example, *Which is **the second biggest** hotel chain / car manufacturer in the world? Where is it based? How many rooms does it have / cars does it sell?*

The six biggest hotel chains ranked by number of rooms	Company	Country	Number of rooms
1	Cendant Corporation	USA	542,630
2	_____	_____	_____
3	Marriott International	USA	_____
4	Accor	France	354,652
5	_____	_____	_____
6	Best Western	_____	313,247

Top six car manufacturers in the world ranked by sales	Company	Country	Sales (in millions)
1	_____	_____	_____
2	Ford Group	USA	4.83
3	VW Group	_____	4.00
4	_____	_____	_____
5	Daimler Chrysler	Germany	_____
6	Fiat Group	Italy	2.61

> **Grammar link**
> for more on comparatives and superlatives see page 104

2. Now make your own sentences. For example,

   *Microsoft is based in Seattle. It is **the largest** software company in the world.*

   *My company is based in Berlin. Locally, we are **the second largest** provider of Internet services.*

Discussion

3. Work in groups to talk about your hotel experiences. What's the best hotel you have ever stayed in? And the worst? What was good or bad about it?

Acquiring a hotel

Fluency

1. You work for MundiHotel, a global hotel organisation which has an interest in acquiring a hotel in the Milan area of Italy for its European chain. There are two existing hotels for sale – the Marco Polo and the Canova – or you could build a new hotel. Look at the table on page 37. Work with a partner and decide which is the best option for your company. Fill in the details for the new hotel, if necessary. Before you begin think about the arguments in favour of each option.

2. Then write a report about your decision. Use the framework below to help you.

   The three options we looked at were ...
   The advantages of the Marco Polo are ...
   On the other hand, ...
   The Canova ...

   However, ...
   The third option is ...
   In conclusion, ...

7 Making comparisons

Name of hotel	Marco Polo	Canova	(new hotel)
Total investment	$23,000,000	$15,000,000	$17-23,000,000
Description	Luxury accommodation. Modern building situated in city centre.	Restored castle dating from Roman times set in 5000m² of countryside with golf course nearby. 10kms from airport.	Land to build a hotel 2kms from airport. Possibly an excellent opportunity.
Annual revenue	$3,700,000	$2,700,000	$3,700,000 (?)
Number of rooms	178	124	approx 200
Average occupancy rate	55%	65%	_____
Swimming pool	No	Yes	_____
Meeting rooms	Yes	Yes	_____
Laundry rooms	Yes	Yes	_____
Spa/sauna	No	Yes	_____
Restaurant	Yes	Yes	_____
Exercise facilities	No	Yes	_____
Car park	Yes	Yes	_____

Room service

1   7.2 It is ten o'clock at night. A guest calls room service to ask for something. Complete the conversation below. Then listen and compare your answers.

Room Service Room service. My name is Johan. Can I help you?
Guest Yes, this is room 301. _____ an early morning call, please?
Room Service Certainly, sir. What time _____ the call?
Guest At half past six.
Room Service 6.30. No problem. _____ breakfast sent up to your room?
Guest No, thanks. I _____ it in the dining room.
Room Service The dining room opens for breakfast at 7.30.
Guest Oh, in that case I _____ in my room. Just coffee and a croissant.
Room Service Coffee and a croissant. _____ ?
Guest No, that's all.
Room Service Okay. _____, sir.
Guest Thank you. Good night.

> **Lexis link**
> for more on the vocabulary of hotel services see page 105

2   Practise the conversation in 1 with a partner.

Fluency 3   Work with a partner.

Speaker A You are the room service clerk.

Speaker B Phone room service to make requests for:
- something to eat
- someone to fix the air conditioning
- tomorrow's weather forecast
- someone to dry-clean a tie or a skirt
- help with the modem/data port
- (*your own request*)

Now change roles. Speaker B, you are the room service clerk. Speaker A see page 128.

Conversation skills

8 Did I ever tell you …?

The trouble with telling a good story is that it invariably reminds the other fellow of a bad one. *Sid Caesar*

anecdote /ˈænɪkˌdəʊt/ noun [C] a story that you tell people about something interesting or funny that has happened to you

from Macmillan English Dictionary

1 8.1 Complete the anecdote below with suitable words. Then listen and compare your answers.

  A Look at that car!
  B Yes, it's a real beauty. Porsche 911.
  A Did I ever tell you about the time I had a _____ in a Porsche?
  B No, I don't think so.
  A It was when I _____ a student. I was _____ in Europe and this chap in a Porsche stopped. He took me all the way across Austria. We _____ about 220 kilometres an hour all the way.
  B What about the _____?
  A Well, they _____ us about four times, but this chap just showed some identity card and they waved us on.
  B Was he someone _____, then?
  A I don't know, I didn't ask. I _____ he was some sort of high-ranking official. He didn't talk much, but we *did* get there very quickly.

2 8.2 Look at these sentences from the anecdote in 1.

  It was when I was a student. I was hitch-hiking in Europe.

  Make similar sentences using the prompts below. There are several alternatives. Then listen and compare your answers.

  It was … / I was …
  a while / live / Italy _____
  b before / start / work / here _____
  c after / leave / university _____
  d when / work / ICL _____
  e before / get / married _____
  f just after / children / born _____
  g look / job _____
  h do / Masters / the States _____

I was ...
- **i** study / at Cambridge _____
- **j** work / small company / north _____
- **k** travel / Asia _____
- **l** stay / Continental Hotel / Prague _____

3 8.3 The speaker ends the anecdote in 1 with a comment:

*He didn't talk much, but we **did** get there very quickly.*

*... we **did** get there very quickly* is similar to *we **certainly** got there very quickly.*

Did adds emphasis to the verb *get*.   **Did** is stressed when you speak.

Make similar comments using the following prompts, then listen and compare your answers.
- **a** we / have a good time / cost a fortune
- **b** he / get the job / have to marry the boss' daughter
- **c** we / get there in the end / sit on a bus all day
- **d** I / get a good job / have to leave the country / find one
- **e** she / make a success / business / her husband / leave her
- **f** he / sell more than anyone else / have a heart attack

4 Complete the sentences below. Use *did* for emphasis.
- **a** It was a good car, _____
- **b** I enjoyed the meal, _____
- **c** The conference wasn't very good, _____
- **d** They managed to find a hotel, _____

5 Complete the sentences below so that they make sense.
- **a** _____, but we did ask first.
- **b** _____, but I did send him an e-mail.
- **c** _____, but he did take her out to dinner.
- **d** _____, but she did give him the job.

6 Work with a partner and each tell an anecdote based on the questions below. Help your partner by asking more questions.

Speaker A
Have you ever been stopped by the police when you were driving? Where were you going? Why did they stop you? Were they right or wrong? What was the outcome? Did it change your attitude either to driving or to the police, or did it confirm what you already thought?

Speaker B
Who was your least favourite teacher at school or lecturer at university? Why didn't you like them? Can you remember an incident that was typical of that person? Who was involved? What happened? What was the outcome? Did it change your point of view in any way or did it confirm what you already thought?

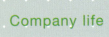

9 Spirit of enterprise

Company life

Beware of all enterprises that require new clothes. *Henry David Thoreau, US writer*

1 Look at the pictures below. They are elements from a story about a successful business. What do you think the business is?

2 🔊 9.1 Listen to a conversation between Simon Taylor, a young entrepreneur, and his bank manager, and see if you are correct.

3 Listen to the conversation again and answer the questions.

   a What does Simon Taylor want to do? _____
   b How does his bank manager react? _____
   c How would you react if you were the bank manager?

4 🔊 9.2 Read the introduction to an article about this story. Before writing the article, the journalist interviewed Simon Taylor about his worm farm. Listen to the interview and answer the questions below.

   a Was the worm farm Simon's first idea? _____
   _____
   b Why did he decide to set up a worm farm? _____
   c What does he mainly feed the worms? _____
   _____
   d Has he tried any other types of food? What? _____
   _____
   e Has it been successful? _____
   f Is his business ecological? _____
   _____

THE WORM MAN

Picture the scene. You go to your bank manager and ask him for money to develop a great business idea – a worm farm. Not surprisingly, the bank manager finds it difficult to keep a straight face. But this isn't an imaginary tale. It's the true story of a business success ...

5 Listen again. Prepare to explain the connections between the following words and phrases.

   a fish farming   investment

   Simon thought about fish farming at first, but decided that the initial investment was too high.

   b worm farming   start-up costs
   _____
   _____

40 9 Spirit of enterprise

c growing demand   toxic waste from the paper industry
   _____
   _____

   d 10 tons   20 tons   250 tons
   _____
   _____

6 What other unusual ways of making money have you heard of?

Present Perfect & Past Simple

7 Number the parts of the summary of Simon's story in the correct order. Check your answers by comparing it with the full article on page 128.
- ☐ Four years ago, Simon ...
- ☐ ... thought about fish farming but the investment ...
- ☐ ... to double production next year. UK fishermen use around 250 tons of worms a year, so ...
- ☐ ... has started to experiment with industrial waste from the paper industry. This year he ...
- ☐ ... acquired some land on his family's farm. At first he ...
- ☐ ... was too high, so he ...
- ☐ ... has produced over ten tons of worms but he expects ...
- ☐ ... opted for a worm farm. He feeds the worms on salad waste from supermarkets but demand ...
- ☐ ... has grown and he ...
- ☐ ... has experimented with other possibilities. For example, he ...
- ☐ ... there is plenty of demand. But he is also looking at other uses.

8 Underline four examples of the Past Simple and four examples of the Present Perfect in 7. Which structure is used to show that:
- a stage in Simon's project is completely finished? _____
- an event is part of a continuing stage in the project? _____

9 Use the word prompts to reconstruct the conversation between Simon and the journalist. Think carefully about which tense you should use.

Journalist this / first idea / for / business?
Simon no / first / think / fish farming
Journalist why / change / mind
Simon decide / investment too big / not want / take / risk
Journalist why / decide / set up / worm farm?
Simon because / start-up costs / relatively low
Journalist how / start?
Simon begin / packing worms / pots / fishermen
Journalist what / feed / worms?
Simon feed / waste / supermarkets & restaurants / demand / grow / we / try other food sources
Journalist example?
Simon we / feed / waste / paper industry
Journalist really / work?
Simon yes / results / very positive / they / recycle / waste / cheaper / burying it / expensive dumps / good / environment
Journalist sound / amazing / how much / produce?
Simon this year / produce / 10 tons / next year / hope / double production / 20
Journalist market / all these worms?
Simon in the UK fishermen use / 250 tons / year / also / look / at other uses

Grammar link
for more on the Present Perfect and Past Simple see page 106

Change

1 Label each graph with two verbs from the box which describe change.

| go up | fall | remain stable | go down | increase | not change |

a b c

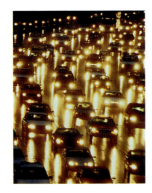

2 Work in groups. Using the verbs in 1, describe what has happened recently in your country or region, and in the company you work for. Use the topics below to help you. For example: *Interest rates **have fallen** in the last six months. The number of people working in my team at work **has increased** recently.*

in your country or region
house prices   taxes
rate of inflation   interest rates
unemployment   population
economic growth   traffic

in your company
number of staff
revenues
profits
amount of work

Has anything else important happened in your country, region or company?

3 Read the information below about a successful Spanish company, Inditex, and answer the questions.

  a Who is the founder of the Inditex Group? _____
  b Where and when did it start? _____
  c What business is it in? _____
  d What is the secret of its success? _____
  e How many companies are there in the group? _____

> **Lexis link**
> for work on word building see page 107

BUSINESS BRIEFING

INDITEX

The founder of Inditex, Amancio Ortega, has a catch phrase: 'Don't explain how we're going to make money today. Tell me how we're going to make it in five years' time.' The Inditex Group's first Zara shop opened its doors in 1975 in La Coruña, Spain. Today, the Group's stores can be seen in places such as New York's 5th Avenue, Paris' Champs-Elysées, London's Regent Street, and Tokyo's Shibuya Shopping Quarters. Its unique management methods, based on innovation and flexibility, have turned Inditex into one of the world's largest fashion groups, made up of almost a hundred companies dealing with activities related to textile design, production and distribution.

Adapted from www.inditex.com

4 Work with a partner. Speaker A look at the instructions below. Speaker B look at the instructions on page 133.

Speaker A Look at the information in the table on page 43. Work with your partner to complete the missing information and find out how Inditex has changed over the last four years.

Inditex	four years ago	now
Shops worldwide		1,377
Shops in Spain		818
Shops in rest of world		559
Countries where the group operates		39
Chains in group		Zara, Pull & Bear, Massimo Dutti, Bershka, Stradivarius, Oysho
Net revenues		€3,249 million
Net profits		€345 million
Headquarters		New building in Arteixo, La Coruña

5 Complete the report using information from 4 and the verbs in the box in either the Past Simple or Present Perfect.

> open   increase   make   move   reach   grow   launch

> The recent history of Inditex is a tremendous success story. Over the last four years the group (a) _____ enormously. It now operates in (b) _____ countries, and the number of shops worldwide (c) _____ from (d) _____ to (e) _____. In this time the group (f) _____ (g) _____ new chains, and (h) _____ 329 new shops in Spain and 300 in the rest of the world. This year net revenues (i) _____ a level of (j) _____, and the group (k) _____ profits of (l) _____. All Inditex's activities are controlled from Arteixo, La Coruña, where the group recently (m) _____ into new headquarters.

6 Write a similar report about the changes in a company you know about.

Work issues

10 Stressed to the limit

> Stress is like having one foot on the accelerator of a car, with the other foot on the brake. We wind up stripping our gears. The chronic build-up of stress takes an enormous toll on our bodies in terms of wear and tear. *Dr Reed C Moskowitz*

Discussion

1   Work with a partner. Which of these factors produce the most stress? Add your own ideas.

> dealing with the public   working long hours   meeting deadlines
> travelling   making phone calls   learning to use new technology
> being promoted   looking after children   doing boring, repetitive tasks
> dealing with big sums of money   being responsible for people's lives
> waiting for other people to do things

2   **10.1** An interviewer for the radio programme *Work Today* spoke to four people in the street about stress. Listen to the interviews and answer the questions.

		Interview 1	Interview 2	Interview 3	Interview 4
a	What does the speaker do?				
b	Does the speaker suffer from stress?				
c	What causes the stress, according to the speaker?				
d	Does the speaker mention any of the reasons in 1? Which?				

3   The last speaker says that stress is more a problem of mental attitude than what you do. Do you agree?

4   In your opinion, what are the three most stressful jobs? Use the list below to help you.

> middle manager   chief executive   teacher   taxi driver   telephonist
> secretary   police officer   factory worker   pilot   air traffic controller
> stockbroker   doctor   lawyer   shop assistant   accountant   waiter
> computer programmer   firefighter   miner   architect   journalist

Now compare your ideas with the list on page 129. Are you surprised? What do you think are the least stressful jobs?

have to

5   For each set of prompts a–g, make at least two sentences with *has to/have to/doesn't have to/don't have to*. For example:

> air traffic controller   factory worker   take decisions   be creative

*An air traffic controller **has to** take decisions very quickly.* (It's necessary)

*A factory worker **doesn't have to** be creative.* (It's not necessary)

44   10 Stressed to the limit

a lawyer   secretary   wear a suit   type letters
___
___

b middle managers   chief executives   solve day-to-day problems   take strategic decisions
___
___

c shop assistant   computer programmer   deal with the public   know computer languages
___
___

d lorry driver   taxi driver   drive long distances   memorise street maps
___
___

e nurse   factory worker   wear special clothes   work at night
___
___

f accountant   telephonist   use a computer   be honest
___
___

g teacher   engineer   tell people what to do   wear a tie
___
___

Make sentences about the other jobs in 3

6 Now interview someone about their job like this:
In your job do you have to ...?   No, but I have to ... / Yes, and I also have to ...

10 Stressed to the limit

Lexis link

for more on the vocabulary of stress at work see page 109

7 You are going to read an article about stress. All the words and phrases on the left are in the article. Match them to the definitions on the right.

a linked to
b root cause of
c overwork
d staff turnover
e makes business sense
f performance-related pay
g morale

1 doing too much work
2 is good for the company
3 principal reason for
4 connected to
5 money for getting better results
6 people joining and leaving a company
7 positive or negative attitude

a	b	c	d	e	f	g

8 In your opinion, are the sentences below true or false? True False

a Stress is always a bad thing.
b Work-related stress can cause health problems.
c Bad management is the main cause of stress.
d Reducing stress costs companies money.
e It's easy for companies to reduce stress.

9 Read the article below. Does the writer agree with your opinions in 8?

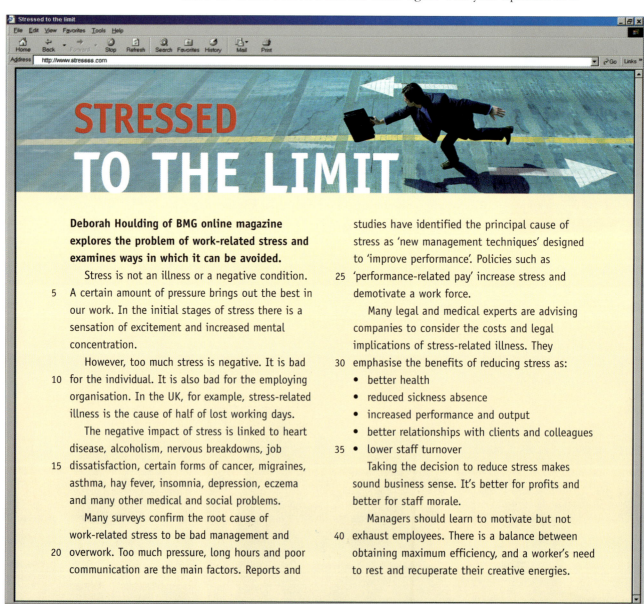

STRESSED TO THE LIMIT

Deborah Houlding of BMG online magazine explores the problem of work-related stress and examines ways in which it can be avoided.

Stress is not an illness or a negative condition. A certain amount of pressure brings out the best in our work. In the initial stages of stress there is a sensation of excitement and increased mental concentration.

However, too much stress is negative. It is bad for the individual. It is also bad for the employing organisation. In the UK, for example, stress-related illness is the cause of half of lost working days.

The negative impact of stress is linked to heart disease, alcoholism, nervous breakdowns, job dissatisfaction, certain forms of cancer, migraines, asthma, hay fever, insomnia, depression, eczema and many other medical and social problems.

Many surveys confirm the root cause of work-related stress to be bad management and overwork. Too much pressure, long hours and poor communication are the main factors. Reports and studies have identified the principal cause of stress as 'new management techniques' designed to 'improve performance'. Policies such as 'performance-related pay' increase stress and demotivate a work force.

Many legal and medical experts are advising companies to consider the costs and legal implications of stress-related illness. They emphasise the benefits of reducing stress as:
• better health
• reduced sickness absence
• increased performance and output
• better relationships with clients and colleagues
• lower staff turnover

Taking the decision to reduce stress makes sound business sense. It's better for profits and better for staff morale.

Managers should learn to motivate but not exhaust employees. There is a balance between obtaining maximum efficiency, and a worker's need to rest and recuperate their creative energies.

10 Complete the chart with the correct form of the word.

noun	verb	adjective
stress	stress	_____ /stressed
motivation	_____	motivating/_____
creation/_____	create	_____
_____	excite	_____ /excited

11 Complete each sentence with one of the words from above.

a Working with the public can be very _____.

b When the new boss arrived, staff morale was very low and nobody was very _____.

c I'm a graphic designer so my job requires a lot of _____.

d I don't find the new project very _____.

12 Make similar sentences about your own company.

Should/shouldn't

13 Look at these sentences.

*Managers **should** recognise their mistakes.* (It's a good idea.)
*Employees **shouldn't** work under unnecessary pressure.* (It's not a good idea.)

Make sentences that are true for you using *should/shouldn't* and the prompts below. For example, work well / have a certain amount of pressure

To work well you should have a certain amount of pressure.

a companies / try / reduce the level of stress
_____

b workers / work very long hours
_____

c managers / communicate / ideas
_____

d companies / invest money / improve conditions
_____

e managers / learn / motivate workers
_____

f workers / have time / rest
_____

Grammar link

for more on *have to* and *should* see page 108

10 Stressed to the limit 47

14 Make sentences about your company like this:

In my company ... should / shouldn't ... but often / in fact they/he/she/we ...

Include the ideas below and add your own.
- distribution of work
- communications
- performance-related pay
- sufficient training
- new technology

The consultant's report

You are going to write a report on a company with problems. Follow steps 1–4 below.

Step 1

Work with a partner. Create your own company.
a What line of business is the company in?
b What's the name of the company?
c Where is it located?
d Is it an old-fashioned or a modern company?
e How long has it existed?

Step 2

You are going to perform a roleplay with a new partner. First, with your original partner, decide who is the employee and who is the consultant. Then find a new partner who is playing a different role to you.

Employee You work for the company you invented. You are completely negative about every aspect of your job and company. Criticise everything and everybody.

Consultant You are a management consultant hired to interview the staff of the employee's company to assess the levels of stress and morale. Interview the employee and note down the answers. Ask questions about

- working hours
- training provided
- internal communication
- company organisation
- holidays
- pay
- (*your own ideas*)

Step 3

Work with your original partner from Step 1. Write a report of the management consultant's interview. Use the framework below or adapt it to suit the interview.

- According to ... the main cause/s of stress in his/her work is/are ...
- Communications in the company are ...
- The system of payment is ...
- With regard to training, the situation is ...
- Other causes of problems are ...
- To reduce the level of stress the company should ...
- In conclusion, ...

MQSC consulting

Interview report

Company:

Name of Interviewee:

Interviewer:

Date:

Step 4

Work with your partner from Step 2 again. Check that the report of your interview is accurate.

Company life

11 Top jobs

If two men on the same job agree all the time, then one is useless. If they disagree all the time, then both are useless. Darryl F Zanuck, US film producer

Present Perfect for unfinished past

1 Read the information about Shimano. Complete it using the words in the box.

| opens   enters   incorporates   manufactures   sets up   celebrates   moves   founds |

BRIEF HISTORY

SHIMANO

1921 Shozaburo Shimano _____ the Shimano Iron Works to produce bicycle components.
1936 Shimano _____ to present-day headquarters in Sakai City, Osaka.
1957 _____ first bicycle gears.
1971 _____ factory in Düsseldorf. Produces first Dura-Ace components for racing bikes.
1972 _____ market for fishing equipment. Launches first specific components for mountain biking – Shimano Deore XT.
1997 _____ Action Sports Division to produce new products for snowboarding.
1999 Launches first products for golf market under the name Ultegra.
2001 _____ 80th anniversary.
2002 _____ hydraulic brake system in the XTR top mountain bike range.

2 Complete the sentences about Shimano using the verbs in the boxes.

| still produces   has produced   started to produce |

+ a Shimano _____ bicycle components in 1921.
+ b It _____ bicycle components today.
= c It _____ bicycle components since 1921.

| has had   still has   opened |

+ d Shimano _____ a factory in Düsseldorf over 30 years ago.
+ e It _____ a factory in Düsseldorf today.
= f It _____ a factory in Düsseldorf for over 30 years.

11 Top jobs 49

3 Match the sentences in 2 to the tenses below.

☑ ☐ Past Simple ☐ ☐ Present Simple ☐ ☐ Present Perfect

4 Make similar sentences about Shimano with these prompts using the Present Perfect, *since* and *for*.

a have / headquarters / Sakai City
___

b manufacture / bicycle gears
___

c make / fishing equipment
___

d produce / components / mountain bikes
___

e have / snowboarding / products division
___

f be / in the golf equipment market
___

Since & for

5 Put the following time expressions in the correct column.

| five minutes   last year   1945   20 years   a long time   I was born   yesterday |
| he arrived   months   a few years   5 o'clock   this morning   a couple of days |

since	for

Grammar link

for more on the Present Perfect see page 110

6 Write sentences which are true for you. Use the Present Perfect, *since* and *for*.

Tell me more

How long

1 Make questions with 'you' using the prompts. Use the Present Simple, Past Simple and Present Perfect, as appropriate.

a What kind of car / have? How long / have / it? Why / choose it?
___
___

b have / a mobile phone? How long / have / it? use it / a lot?
___
___

c Where / live? How long / live / there?
___

d Where / work? How long / work / there? What / job?
___

e How long / have / present job? Like / it?
___

f know
___

g be interested in
___

2 Work with a partner. Ask and answer the questions in 1. Try to get more information about each subject, if you can.

3 Change partners. Tell each other about your previous partner. For example:
Lucien lives just outside Toulouse. He has lived there for three years. He works as a research scientist at the university. He's worked there since last June.

Bill's friend

1 ▭ 11.1 The words and phrases below are from a radio profile of Steve Ballmer, the CEO of Microsoft. Listen to the profile and number the words in the order you hear them.

☐ deadline ☐ sales and support ☐ Proctor and Gamble
☐ chief executive ☐ chairman ☐ wealthiest man
☐ first business manager ☐ wedding ☐ basketball

2 Read the script of the radio profile and correct the ten mistakes. Then listen again and check your answers.

BILL AND STEVE – two men and a destiny

Who is the boss of the world's leading manufacturer of personal and business computing software? Ask most people and they will say the mega rich Bill Gates. But no, the planet's wealthiest man stepped down from the top job in January 2000 to take on a new appointment and pursue what he claims is his real passion. Apparently this is not making money, but his art collection. Since then, the chief executive of Microsoft Corporation has been his old university chum, Steve Ballmer.

History tells us that Gates dropped out of Yale to set up Microsoft with Paul Allen in 1975. Meanwhile, his other friend Steve, who lived down the hall, graduated with a degree in social science. He then went on to work for two years at Proctor and Gamble, and attend the Manchester University Graduate School of Business.

Ballmer has worked for Microsoft since 1980, when Gates remembered his college mate and hired him as the company's first business manager. Over the last 20 years Ballmer has been in charge of several Microsoft divisions, including operations, marketing, and sales and support. In July 1998 he was promoted to managing director, a role that gave him day-to-day responsibility for running the company. However, since Gates became 'Chief Software Architect', Ballmer has assumed full management control of Microsoft. (Just in case, Bill has retained some power as Chairman.)

Legend has it that in spring 1986, soon after hiring Ballmer, Gates called him into his office. Microsoft's deadline to produce Office 97 was getting behind schedule, and Gates reportedly threatened to fire his friend if the software wasn't on the shelves by the end of the year. Needless to say, Windows was ready by the end of the year, and they have remained the best of friends. Proof of this is that Steve was godfather at Bill's wedding.

Ballmer has influenced Microsoft with his own brand of energy and discipline. He says, 'I want everyone to share my passion for cats and dogs. I want people to understand the amazing, positive way our software can make leisure time more enjoyable, and businesses more successful.' Ballmer plays squash and loves basketball.

3 Underline three examples of the Present Perfect in the script which tell us when a present situation started.

4 How much of the script can you remember without looking? Use the words in 1 to reconstruct the story with a partner.

Vocabulary

5 Find words and phrases in the script in 2 which mean the same as the following:
- **a** resign/leave a job _____
- **b** found/establish _____
- **c** finish a university course _____
- **d** university qualification _____
- **e** employ _____
- **f** responsible for _____
- **g** give someone a better job _____
- **h** dismiss or sack _____
- **i** spare time _____

6 Use the words and phrases in 5 to complete the following sentences.
- **a** If they _____ you, you'll get more money.
- **b** He _____ the company with the money he got from his family.
- **c** Who is _____ marketing at the company?
- **d** Last year the company _____ 350 new production line workers.
- **e** John _____ from Oxford with a degree in economics.
- **f** She has an MBA as well as a _____ in law.
- **g** They _____ her because she wasn't doing her job properly.
- **h** The managing director _____ after the financial scandal.
- **i** With this new job I don't have much _____, and I miss being able to do sport.

> **Lexis link**
>
> for more on the vocabulary of company news see page 111

7 Write sentences which are true for you using the words and phrases in 6.

Headhunters

1   11.2 Peter Davis is in the office when he receives an unexpected call from John Lindsay. Listen to the conversation and answer the questions.

   a   Why does John Lindsay call Peter Davis?

   b   When did Peter Davis start work for Blueprint International?

   c   What did he do before?

   d   How long has he been in charge of the international division?

   e   When did he get married?

   f   Has he got any children?

   g   Is he interested in what the caller has to say?

Discussion   2   Discuss the following questions with other people in the class.

   a   What type of management consultants does John Lindsay work for?

   b   Do you think what he does is ethical?
   c   How would you react in this situation?

Fluency   3   Interview your partner about his/her career history and make notes. Ask questions about work, education, home, family and possessions. Use the prompts in the box to help you.

> How long have you …?   When / Where did you … before?
> When did you start / leave / finish …?

Writing   4   Using your notes, write a report for *People Search* on your partner. Use the model below.

> Peter Davis has worked for Blueprint International since 1997 where he has been head of their International Division for three years. Before Blueprint International he was at Navigate for three years. This was his first job after university where he studied engineering. He graduated from Nottingham University in 1993. He has been married for two years and has one child.

11 Top jobs

Conversation skills

12 Conversation gambits

> The things most people want to know about are usually none of their business.
> George Bernard Shaw

gambit /ˌɡæmbɪt/ noun [C] something you say or do in an attempt to gain an advantage

from *Macmillan English Dictionary*

1 Read the article about a type of bar and think about the following questions. Then discuss them with a partner.

   a Do you think the Remote Lounge is a good idea?
   b Are there bars like this where you live?
   c Do you express yourself better by e-mail/on the Internet or face to face?
   d If you were travelling alone, would you go to a bar like this?

REMOTELOUNGE

The Remote Lounge, located in the heart of downtown Manhattan, helps its clients to break the ice. For those who find it hard to take the first step, the Remote Lounge provides an innovative solution. Customers can 'spy' on other customers, as well as be 'spied' on themselves. The Remote Lounge offers its clients sixty cameras and
5 a hundred video screens. Individual consoles allow the customer to see who else is in the bar, order a drink, or send a message to another stranger, all without being seen. They can also take pictures which later appear on the bar's website.

According to the owners, in this situation their customers feel less shy about talking to someone they don't know. The person on the receiving end of a message can reject it, of
10 course, but they usually choose to continue the conversation using the console's telephone handset. The owners say that people using the Internet have learned to express themselves with greater freedom, using e-mail and chat rooms. They claim to have applied the same concept to their bar.

In the Remote Lounge, which officially opened on October 9th 2001, and is now open
15 seven days a week from 6 pm to 4 am, it's difficult to spend an evening staring at your glass of beer.

Introducing yourself

2 🔊 **12.1** You are at a conference and you don't know anybody. What can you say to start a conversation with someone? Listen and complete the four conversations below.

1 A Excuse me, _____ the ITM conference?
   B Yes, that's right.
   A Me too. _____
   B I think it's over there.
   A Oh, yes. Right, I'm Paulo, _____
   B Hello, Paulo, I'm Kate. _____

2 A Phew! _____
   B Yes, they always seem to have the heating on full.
   A So, it's not _____
   B No, it's my fourth time here.
   A Oh, right, so _____. I'm Boris.
   B David. _____

3 A Is it _____, or is there some problem with coverage here?
   B Oh, _____. No, mine seems _____ okay.
   A Typical, flat batteries and nowhere to charge up.
   B _____
   A Oh, _____, but I was expecting a call on this number.
   B I see.
   A _____ Nadine, by the way. From Xanadu Electronics.
   B Pleased to meet you. I'm Miko.

4 A Excuse me, _____
   B No, I'm sorry, I don't.
   A _____
   B Oh, here. _____
   A Thanks. By the way, I'm Bill Smart from Silicon Technologies.
   B Right, _____? I'm Kazuo Yamada from Lexico.

Starting a conversation

3 Allan Vilkas is having a quiet drink in a hotel in Dublin after dinner. The other customer in the bar has a newspaper, but he's not reading it. What do you think Allan says to begin a conversation?

4 🔊 **12.2** Complete the conversation using the phrases in the box. Then listen and check your answers.

> finished with it   your time   if I had a quick look at   here on
> to check out   go ahead   the way

Allan Excuse me, would you mind _____ your newspaper?
Stranger Er, no, _____. I've _____.
Allan There's just something I want _____.
Stranger No problem. Take _____.
Allan Thanks. By _____, my name's Allan. I'm _____ a business trip.
Stranger Oh, right.

12 Conversation gambits 55

5 🔊 **12.3** Now Allan has the newspaper. Giving it back is another excuse to begin a conversation. Which of the following do you think he does?

  a mention the political situation
  b comment on the weather forecast
  c say something about sport
  d invite the other person for a drink

  Listen to find out.

6 In first meetings, people often ask each other some of the following questions. Reorganise the words to make questions. Then match them to the answers 1–10. There are two possible answers for each question.

  a you where are from
  Where are you from? _____ 1 ☐

  b been have long you how here
  _____ ☐ ☐

  c long staying how are you
  _____ ☐ ☐

  d think what you Dublin do of
  _____ ☐ ☐

  e business here you on are
  _____ ☐ ☐

  1 I'm from Turkey.
  2 Until Friday.
  3 Another four or five days.
  4 It seems very nice.
  5 I've been here for a couple of days now.
  6 Yes. I'm visiting some customers.
  7 I come from South Africa.
  8 It's a bit cold for me.
  9 Since Saturday.
  10 Yes. I'm here to buy some machinery.

7 🔊 **12.4** Listen to the conversation. Which of the questions and answers in 6 do the speakers use? Circle them.

Conversation topics

8 The two men in the conversation in 7 talk about football and golf. Sport is a 'safe' topic. What other topics are safe? Which should you avoid? Circle the safe topics.

> cars   religion   politics and the state of the world   personal life
> business   the stock exchange   money and personal finance
> the weather   art   music   local attractions   the opposite sex

Saying goodbye

9 12.5 Complete the conversation. Then listen and compare your answers.

Sean Oh, well, Allan, it's getting late. I have to _____. Thanks for the _____, and good luck with your _____.

Allan Right, it was nice _____.

Sean It was nice to _____. Cheerio, then.

Allan Bye.

10 When Sean wants to end the conversation, he says *It's getting late. I have to be off*. Match the parts of the sentences below to make other ways to end a conversation.

a Excuse me, but I've just ...
b I think they're going ...
c Excuse me, but I think ...
d Mm, that's interesting. Excuse me, but, ...
e Hang on a minute, but I think I have ...
f Sorry to cut you off, but I arranged ...

1 ... a call on my mobile. I'll catch you later.
2 ... someone is trying to catch my attention.
3 ... do you know where the toilets are?
4 ... seen someone I have to talk to.
5 ... to start. I'll see you later.
6 ... to meet someone at the bar five minutes ago.

Fluency

11 Work with a partner. Look at the headlines below. Imagine you borrowed your partner's newspaper and you are now giving it back. Start a conversation about one of the headlines. Maintain the conversation as long as possible. Start like this: *Thank you for the newspaper. Have you seen this article about ...?*

- Prime Minister says economic situation 'hopeless'
- Scientists discover link between golf and IQ
- Mobiles banned on public transport
- UK to drive on right
- Dog wins lottery
- Intelligent life discovered on Mars
- Princess Diana alive and living in New Jersey
- US President consults private astrologer

Connecting

13 Air travel

If God had meant us to fly, he would have given us wings. Common saying

Discussion

1 Discuss the following questions with other people in the class.
   a How often do you fly?
   b What things can go wrong when you travel by air?
   c Have you had any bad flying experiences?
   d For you, which is the best seat – near the front or back, an aisle seat, a window seat or the one in the middle?

2 13.1 Listen to the conversation. Which seat does the passenger get? Circle it on the seating plan on the left.

3 Complete the conversation using the words in the box. Listen again and check your answers, if necessary.

| aisle | passport | laptop | allowed | boarding pass | check in | exit |
| gate | pack | left | available | busy | | |

Check-in clerk Good morning.

Passenger Hello. Is this where I _____ for flight BA 264?

Check-in clerk Yes. Can I see your _____, please? Thank you. Did you _____ your bags yourself, sir?

Passenger Yes. Excuse me, but apart from my _____ I only have this small bag. Is it okay if I take it on as hand luggage?

Check-in clerk Well, officially, you're only _____ one piece of hand luggage, but it's not a large bag, is it? So, that's all right, I suppose.

Passenger Thanks very much. Could I have an _____ seat, please, near the front? Or a window seat?

Check-in clerk I'm sorry, the flight's quite _____. There are no window or aisle seats _____.

Passenger Oh … could you show me where the _____ seats are?

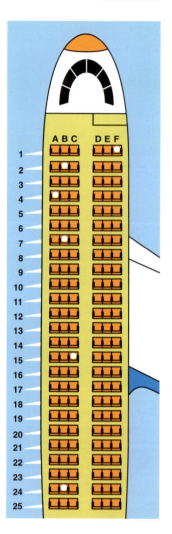

58   13 Air travel

Check-in clerk Yes, sir. Here, here and here.

Passenger Right, I'll take the one up front near the _____ on the left.

Check-in clerk Okay. Here's your _____. The flight will be boarding at _____ number 23 in 20 minutes. Have a good flight.

Passenger Thanks. Goodbye.

Check-in clerk Goodbye.

Battle of the armrests

1. Read the introduction to an article on avoiding a travel problem. What do you think the 'strategies' are?

> **THE MIDDLE SEAT**
>
> It's happened to everyone – even the most experienced business traveller and frequent flier. A last-minute trip, no seat assignment on the aeroplane and the only seat left on a packed flight? You've guessed it – the middle seat. It can make your trip miserable. Here are some strategies to help you avoid the worst seat.

Conditionals with *will*

2. Look at this 'first conditional' sentence:

Conditions	Consequences
If + present	*will* + infinitive
If you book early,	you'll be able to choose your seat.

or You'll be able to choose your seat if you book early.

Match the conditions to the consequences. Make as many logical combinations as possible.

	Conditions		Consequences
a	if you book months in advance ② 5 6	1	you'll get on and off the plane faster
b	if you sit at the front _____	2	you'll be too early for a seat assignment
c	if you check in late _____	3	you'll have to go to the toilet a lot
d	if you're polite to the check-in attendant _____	4	you'll be able to stretch your legs
e	if you pretend to be ill or pregnant _____	5	you'll sometimes be able to change your seat
f	if you trust your instincts _____	6	you'll get more personal space
g	if you dominate the armrests _____	7	you'll pay for it with an uncomfortable seat
h	if you use your laptop _____	8	you'll choose better seatmates
i	if you drink too much _____	9	you'll feel claustrophobic
j	if you get up during the flight _____	10	you'll feel guilty the entire flight

Grammar link

for more on conditionals with *will* see page 112

3. 13.2 Listen to someone giving advice about getting a good seat. Circle the combinations in 2 which correspond to what the speaker says. Do you agree with the advice?

Discussion

4. Work in groups. Make a list of five *do*s and five *don't*s for business air travellers.

Air rage

1 Look at the headline from a newspaper article. What word do you think is missing?

_____ PASSENGERS GROUNDED

Now read the article.

IMAGINE you are checking in at Heathrow airport and the check-in clerk informs you that you don't have a seat on your flight because of overbooking. Naturally you are upset, but be careful what you say. If you are rude to the ground staff, you will not be allowed to board you flight. Not if you're flying with
5 British Airways, that is.

The company has introduced new rules prohibiting customers from boarding flights if they use 'threatening, abusive or insulting words to ground staff or crew'. The airline claims that last year their staff dealt with over 200 cases of air rage, including minor disagreements over smoking on board, but also more serious
10 incidents involving violent or drunken behaviour. However, check-in staff believe that they can prevent these problems if they deal with difficult passengers before they actually get on the plane.

Owen Highley, a BA lawyer who helped to draw up the new rules, told *The Times* newspaper in London: 'If we think someone is going to be a disruptive passenger,
15 the most obvious thing to do is to deny them boarding. But there has to be common sense. We are not going to ban from flight everybody who gets a bit stroppy.'

A spokeswoman for BA said: 'Some people are understandably angry when they check in if they have missed a connecting
20 flight because of a delay or some other problem. It is only if we fear they could become a danger that we will act.' However, BA will not offer a refund to passengers who are banned from boarding their planes unless they have a fully flexible fare,
25 and those involved in the most serious incidents will get a lifetime ban. You have been warned!

Discussion

2 Sometimes air travel can be very frustrating. Things can go wrong and people get angry. Do you think the BA rules are fair? Do you ever get 'a bit stroppy'?

3 Complete the following sentences, which summarise the rules in the article in 1.

a If _____, they won't be allowed to get on planes.

b There won't be incidents of air rage during flights if _____

c We will deny someone boarding if _____

d If a passenger just gets 'a bit stroppy', _____

e If _____, BA will ban you for life.

4   The verbs in each of the four lists below often accompany the nouns on the right. One verb in each list is wrong. Delete the verb from the wrong list and add it to the correct list.

| receive
miss
book   a flight
board
take
_____ | tackle
introduce   rules
obey
ignore
_____ | claim
catch   a refund
offer
_____ | deal with
solve
give   a problem
break
_____ |

Lexis link

for more on the vocabulary of negotiating and air travel see page 113

5   Use the verb + noun combinations in 4 to complete the sentences below. Then answer the questions in brackets.

a   You should not _____ _____ if you don't think they are sensible. (*Do you agree?*)

b   In my job I have to _____ a lot of _____ every day. (*Is this true for you?*)

c   If I ever need to _____ _____ _____, I always shop around at different travel agents to get the best deal. (*Is this what you do?*)

d   If you buy something that doesn't work, you _____ _____ _____ or get the shop to change it. (*When was the last time you did this?*)

The negotiation game

1   13.3 You are going to play a game in which you have to negotiate the price, quantity, delivery time, payment terms and guarantee period of a product to gain points. Before you play, listen to two people playing the game as an example.

Fluency   2   Work with a partner. First of all, decide what the product is.

Speaker A you are the buyer. Look at the instructions and chart on page 129.
Speaker B you are the seller. Look at the instructions and chart on page 132.

Work issues

14 Hiring and firing

Sack the lot! *Letter to The Times, September 2nd, 1919 (on overmanning and overspending within government departments)*

1 Look at the headline below. What do you think the article is about?

2 Read the article to see if you are correct. Then answer the questions.

IBIZA PHONE-IN PRIZE WINNER FIRED

Nicola Williams, a 31-year-old single mother from Newbridge in South Wales, couldn't believe her luck when she was told she was the winner of a Mediterranean holiday for herself and her six-year-old daughter. The week's break on the sunshine island of Ibiza was the prize in a radio phone-in competition.
She told reporter Hefina Rendle on BBC Wales television that she was 'totally over the moon, really excited'. However, only minutes later she was laid off. Nicola, an electronic parts worker, who phoned the radio station from work using her own mobile phone, was unaware that her boss was standing nearby. He asked her to hang up, took her into his office, and told her she was sacked. She was ordered to leave the factory immediately.
This was her first job since the birth of her daughter, and she was fired by the same manager who originally hired her.
But the story may have a happy ending. The commercial radio station which ran the competition is now trying to find her another job. A spokesman for the station said that people should be allowed to take part in competitions from work, as they are in general life. He said it was sad that the manager couldn't see the good side and just congratulate Nicola on her good luck.
Skytronics, Nicola's former employer, refused to be interviewed by the BBC, and later issued a statement supporting the action of their manager.

a Do you think the sacking was justified?
b Would this be possible in your company, or in your country?
c What advice would you give to Nicola?

3 Find two more verbs in the article that are similar in meaning to 'sack'. Which verb is more formal than the others? _____

The passive

4 Find sentences in the article that are similar in meaning to the following:
   a They laid her off. _____
   b They ordered her to leave the factory immediately.
   _____

5 Compare the two pairs of sentences in 4.
   a Which are active and which are passive? _____
   _____
   b Who is mentioned first in the active sentences? _____
   c Who is mentioned first in the passive sentences? _____
   d Who is the story about? _____
   e What is the advantage of using the passive sentences? _____
   _____
   f The agent in the active sentences is 'they'. What happens to it in the passive sentences? Why? _____
   _____

6 Read the manager's report of the incident in 2. He uses the passive to sound more objective and formal in style. Complete the report using the verbs below in the passive.

> ask   give   note   inform   warn   give   inform

On two occasions in November Ms Nicola Williams, an employee in the assembly plant, (a) _____ that using a mobile phone in work hours was against the company rules. Both these warnings (b) _____ by another supervisor, and (c) _____ in her file. Then, in December, on a further occasion, she (d) _____ a written warning. Finally, On Friday, 12 January at 10.30 I (e) _____ of a problem on the factory floor. When I arrived there, I found a lot of noise and shouting going on. Ms Williams was using her mobile phone to participate in a radio phone-in programme. Apparently she had won a prize. I asked her to put the phone down immediately, and to come in to my office. I decided to terminate her employment, and in the presence of Ms Jones, my deputy, Ms Williams was told that she was being sacked. She became hysterical and abusive, and (f) _____ to leave the factory immediately. She (g) _____ that her possessions would be forwarded to her by post.

7 In what way are the details about the incident different?

_____
_____

8 Improve these short texts by changing one verb to the passive in each one.

  a They have laid off over 35,000 people in the last five years, unemployment is rising, and there are social problems in the region.
  35,000 people have been laid off in the last five years, unemployment is rising, and there are social problems in the region.

  b The business is a great success. They are hiring new staff and it is expanding fast. _____

  c As there was a recession and the number of orders decreased, they closed one of the factories. _____

  d To improve margins, it is making the new model in Hungary where labour costs are lower. _____

  e Ford has several plants in Europe. One of them is in Valencia and it produces the Escort there. _____

  f They have announced plans for the new industrial estate. It will cover ten hectares and create space for over fifteen business ventures. _____

> **Grammar link**
> for more on the passive see page 114

Discussion

9 Work in groups. In what situations do you think sacking is justified? Think about the following:

> dishonesty   punctuality   disrespect to superiors
> not meeting objectives or achieving results   violence   inappropriate dress
> industrial action (going on strike)   revealing company secrets

Add your own ideas, if you like.

Applying for a job

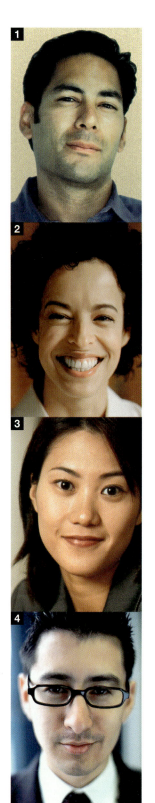

1. **14.1** Listen to four people talking about their approach to applying for a job. Take notes and match the people on the left to the summaries below.

   a I'm looking for a chance to develop and demonstrate my true potential. ☐
   b My qualifications and experience speak for themselves. ☐
   c I'm so brilliant at whatever I do, they would be lucky to have me working in their company. ☐
   d There may be people with better qualifications and experience, but no one is more enthusiastic or hard working than me. ☐

2. Which speaker(s) do you agree with? What approach did you use to get your present job? Does the approach you use depend on the job?

3. Read the following extracts from letters of application. Match them to the summaries in 1.

   ☐ I am very keen to work for your company because of its excellent reputation. I do not have the specific qualifications or experience referred to in your advertisement. However, I am applying because I feel I am able to make up for this through hard work and willingness to learn.

   ☐ If you believe in the pursuit of excellence, then I am interested in joining your company. I set high standards for myself and expect them from others, especially the organisations that I work for. I look forward to an opportunity to add to the list of already outstanding achievements, which are outlined in my CV.

   ☐ From my CV, you will see that five years at a chemicals multinational have given me a solid business background. I am responsible for my department's logistical planning, which has developed my organisational skills. However, I am now looking for opportunities for further development and responsibility, which my present employer cannot offer.

   ☐ As a commercially aware and linguistically trained university graduate, I have a broad range of employment experience at blue-chip companies in both the USA and Europe. I am dynamic and creative, with a strong team spirit and leadership qualities. I have a proven record of working with individuals at all levels through highly developed interpersonal and communication skills.

Reading between the lines

4. Read the extracts in 3 again. There are certain formal phrases people use in letters of application to talk about their qualities and achievements. Underline phrases which mean the following:

   a I'd really like to work for you because you're such a great company.
   b If you think doing things well is important, I'd like to work for you.
   c I don't really have the profile of the ideal candidate.
   d I've worked with many different, important companies.
   e I've shown I can work with all kinds of people and get on with everyone.

f I look after the practical day-to-day aspects of department organisation.
g I want a new job because my company probably won't be able to promote me.
h I have five years of international business experience working for a chemicals company.

5   Use some of the phrases in 3 to write a paragraph introducing your own CV.

A job interview

1   Read the job advert and CV below. Why do you think Sara applied for the job?

INTERNATIONAL SALES MANAGER

Multinational food packaging equipment manufacturer seeks **International Sales Manager** to call on Europe and Latin America. Base $80K and commission, full benefits and expenses. Prefers: fluency in one or more foreign languages. Send resumé with cover letter indicating citizenship and salary requirements.

	Sara Verkade 58, Stoppard Drive, London SW16 Tel: 353 865 344872 E-mail: sara.verkade@gmz.net
Date & place of birth	23.7.78, Maassluis, The Netherlands
Marital status	Single
Nationality	Dutch
Qualifications	September 1996 – July 1999 BComm, Marketing Management, Haagse Hogeschool, The Hague
Employment history	June 2000 – present *Management Team Co-ordinator, Helena Rubinstein, L'Oreal* Organising meetings, events and conferences. Analysing sales figures and producing relevant reports and charts. Customer relations and responding to complaints and queries. **June 1999 – June 2000** *SPC Professional, Sales Productivity Centre, IBM* Sales team support. Research, pricing and proposal-writing on million dollar bids.
Languages	Dutch, English, German, Spanish
IT Skills	Proficient user of Microsoft Office suite

2   **14.2** Sara was interviewed for the job. Listen to the interview. Do you think they employed her?

3   Listen again and complete the phrases below.
   a Now, this is just a preliminary interview to _____ details.
   b Do your present _____ you are?
   c What don't you _____ position?
   d Well, Sara, can I ask you a _____ your CV?
   e Do you, in fact, have any _____ experience?
   f ... an 'SPC professional'. What _____ mean?
   g Yes, we provided _____ twenty salesmen from different sectors of the company.
   h ... it was a position that required a lot of time _____ and prioritising of tasks.
   i I'd like more responsibility and to be able to _____ and my languages.

Lexis link
for more on the vocabulary of procedures see page 115

4   Do you think the interviewer was fair in the interview?

What about the workers?

1. What is happening in the photographs on this page? How do you think these situations relate to employment and staffing?

2. Work with a partner. You will each read an article relating to the employment situation in a country and do three exercises. When you have finished, turn back to this page. Student A see page 127. Student B see page 133.

3. Complete the sentences with words and phrases from the articles in 2. Are the sentences true for you? Discuss them with your partner.

   a. An advanced society should pay _____ to people who can't find work.
   b. The average age of my country's _____ is getting younger.
   c. Flexible labour laws help to reduce the _____.
   d. Using _____ causes job insecurity and lower productivity.
   e. _____ are more important than the interests of big business.
   f. Money and security are the _____ in most people's work.
   g. If the _____ can't find work, they should take any job they are offered.
   h. Companies should invest more in training if they need _____.
   i. It is often hard to predict your _____ needs over a long period.
   j. A good salary doesn't necessarily _____ for a lack of job security.

4. The noun / verb combinations in the box were in the articles in 2. The verbs were in the passive. Can you remember the sentences? Tell your partner.

A	survey / carry out	firms / contact	staff / pay
	salaries / negotiate	conditions / agree	
B	country / bring	strike / call	offers / put
	anyone / sack	reforms / defend	

Discussion

5. Discuss the following questions in relation to your country.

   a. What are the laws about unemployment benefits? Do you think they are fair?
   b. What rights do workers have? How do they affect employment?
   c. Why do you think there is a shortage of skilled workers? Do you think the use of temporary labour is a good solution to the problem?
   d. 'It is increasingly difficult to provide people with jobs for life.' Do you think this is true?

14 Hiring and firing

Work issues

15 Time

> Time, like a loan from the bank, is something you're only given when you possess so much that you don't need it.
>
> *John Braine, British novelist*

Discussion

1 Discuss the following questions with other people in the class.

   a The Pareto Principle, also known as the 80:20 rule, says that 80% of what we produce derives from 20% of our activity. Does this mean that:
   - we should work just one day a week?
   - almost perfect is good enough?
   - most work time is unproductive?
   - something else?

   b A proverb says that 'An hour in the morning is worth two in the evening.' Do you agree?

   c Read the information in the box. Why do you think this is?

> British workers put in the longest hours in Europe. However, they are 25% less productive than the French, and 15% less than the Germans.

Collocations

2 Put vowels in the spaces to complete the verbs below.

   s p _ n d
   s _ v _
   w _ s t _   money
   h _ v _   time
   _ n v _ s t

Vilfredo Pareto, 1848 – 1923

3 Complete the sentences using words from 2. Are they true for you?

   a At work I _____ a lot of time on the phone to people and answering e-mails.

   b I plan my day carefully. If you prepare things well, you can _____ a lot of time.

   c I don't _____ much time for myself, but when I do, I like to get some exercise.

   d Computers are supposed to make you more efficient, but they can also make you _____ a lot of time.

> **Lexis link**
>
> for more on the vocabulary of working conditions see page 117

Discussion

4 Discuss the following questions with a partner.

   a Some people say 'Time is money'. Do you agree?

   b In what ways do you think you waste or save time and money?

   c What are your working hours? If you could choose, how would you organise your working hours?

Time management

1 You are going listen to a talk on time management. The words on the left are from the talk. Match them to the definitions on the right.

a	resource	1	determined
b	assign	2	things which have to be done
c	approach	3	level of importance or urgency
d	ruthless	4	time limits for finishing a job
e	delegated	5	something you need to do a job
f	priority	6	way of doing things
g	tasks	7	given to someone else to do
h	deadlines	8	give

a	b	c	d	e	f	g	h

2 15.1 Listen to the talk and number the speaker's slides in the correct order.

TIME MANAGEMENT
ORGANISE
- Blocks of time
- Deadlines
- Time of day

TIME MANAGEMENT
PRIORITISE
- Important and/or Urgent

TIME MANAGEMENT
ANALYSE
PRIORITISE
ORGANISE

TIME MANAGEMENT
ANALYSE
- Record
- Reduce
- Delegate

3 Explain the slides in your own words.

4 Now read the presentation and complete it using the words in 1. Listen again and check, if necessary.

TECHNIQUES FOR EFFECTIVE TIME MANAGEMENT

Good morning and welcome. I'm here today to talk about time management. My aim is to share some techniques which will help you to use your time more efficiently.

Time is like money, people and equipment. It's a limited (1) _____. Time management is about making the best possible use of it. So, what are the basic concepts of time management? Today we're going to look at three fundamental steps.

The first step is to analyse how you use your time now.

This requires a methodical (2) _____. Break your day into half hour periods. Record what you do in each period.

Look at the list. Ask yourself which (3) _____ were really necessary. Cut everything that isn't necessary. Be (4) _____. Most wasted time is the result of unquestioned activity.

Take a look at the necessary tasks. Could someone else do them? Never do work yourself that can be safely (5) _____. Other people may not perform the task as well as you. But without experience they'll never learn.

The next step is to prioritise.

Take the tasks which genuinely require your attention and put them in order of (6) _____ – which are the most important, which are urgent needs.

Lastly, organise your time and your tasks.

Ask yourself 'How much time will I need?' Be realistic because work tends to expand to fill the time available.

Set realistic (7) _____. The right amount of pressure brings speed and high performance, but on the other hand, too much pressure means things can go wrong.

When possible, organise your work so as to have large blocks of time for top priority tasks like problem analysis and forward planning. Discover the time of day when you are at your best and (8) _____ the most difficult tasks to it.

So, analyse, prioritise, organise. Now I'd like to look at what this means in more detail ...

Collocations

5 Without looking back at the text, match the words to make seven collocations.

a	assign	_____	approach
b	be	_____	deadlines
c	delegate	_____	priority
d	limited	_____	resource
e	methodical	_____	ruthless
f	set	_____	tasks
g	top	_____	tasks

Discussion

6 How well do you manage your time? Complete the 'You' column with approximate percentages for the time you spend on the different activities. Add other activities, if necessary. Then complete the 'Your partner' column by asking *How much time do you spend on ...?* Then change round.

Activity	You	Your partner
planning & delegating		
meetings		
correspondence		
telephoning		
reading		
dealing with problems		
_____		
_____		
	100%	100%

What differences are there between the way you and your partner manage your time? Why do you think this is?

7 Complete the descriptions of two types of manager using the words in the box. Then look at page 129 to check your answers. Which kind of manager are you?

> meetings emergency busy problems suppliers delegates administration

The busy manager

His life is not planned. Perhaps that is why he is _____. His use of time indicates an entirely responsive approach to his job, with more time devoted to _____ than customer service. The high level of _____ shows there are serious problems.

The effective manager

She _____ correspondence to subordinates and deals with major issues herself or by telephone. Her _____ are well planned. She is popular with customers and _____ because she gets to know them well and her reading makes her knowledgeable. She doesn't just discuss _____; she solves them.

Just in time

1 Read the article and answer the questions below.

a How did they try life without time? _____

b What was the aim of the experiment? _____

c Why do companies use time as a measure of productivity? _____

d Why is the normal working timetable (nine to five) inefficient? _____

e What was the result of the experiment? _____

Life without time

How dependent are we on time? Is life without clocks less stressful? One company decided to find out. If you really want to know how dependent you are on time, try removing your watch for a day and count how many times you find yourself looking at your bare wrist. At AOL they decided to take the experiment one step further by taking away all the clocks at their UK headquarters and covering the time displays on computers with tape. Then they told everybody to carry on working as usual.

The idea was to investigate how pressure of time can lead to stress, and to see how a clockless environment would affect productivity and workflow. After all, they say that time is money and it is true that companies use time to control their activities because it is easy to measure. But humans have a biological clock which doesn't necessarily correspond to the standard eight-hour working day. We are more productive in the morning and then our efficiency tends to drop off after lunch. So, if you're feeling hungry, why not have something to eat instead of waiting for the lunch break? Or, if you're finished your work, don't hang on until it's time to clock off, just go home. (Yes, but what if it's time to go home and you haven't finished your work? asks the boss!)

So, what happens when we rely on our internal body clock instead of artificial deadlines? According to one worker, 'Most people carried on as normal although some took advantage of the opportunity to have an early lunch.' Another said 'This is ideal. It makes sense to be able to work when you need to and leave the office when you don't.' On the other hand, one secretary found the experience 'disorientating. We have a fixed routine and it's difficult to change habits.'

However, one office manager was in no doubt: 'Thank goodness we are going to bring the clocks back tomorrow. Make no mistake, a clockless office leads to chaos. Some people may be less stressed without clocks, but you need to know where people are and when, and meetings, for example, can last forever if you don't have a time limit.'

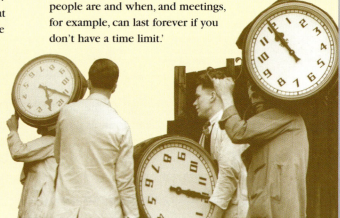

2 Discuss the following questions.

a What do you think of this experiment? Is it useful, interesting, or a waste of time?
b How aware do you need to be of time in your job?
c Could you work without a watch or clocks?
d Do you have lunch etc. at the same time every day?

Vocabulary **3** Find words and phrases in the article which mean the same as the following:

a continue _____
b fall quickly _____

c result in _____
d wait _____
e quantify _____

4 Use the words and phrases in 3 to complete the following sentences.
  a Time management methods _____ to unnecessary stress.
  b In some businesses it is difficult to _____ efficiency.
  c When you have to make a decision, it's best to _____ until the last minute.
  d If you _____ in the same job for a long time, you lose interest.
  e The amount of activity in an office _____ on a Friday afternoon.

5 Which of the sentences in 4 do you agree with?

Going to

6 Look at this sentence from the article on page 70 and answer the questions.
  *Thank goodness we **are going to** bring the clocks back tomorrow.*
  a Does the sentence refer to the past, present or future? _____
  b Which of the following is closest in meaning to 'we **are going to** bring the clocks back'?
   • We would like to bring the clocks back ...
   • We are intending to bring the clocks back ...
   • We have to bring the clocks back ...

7 Plan how you are going to spend your next working day. Then explain your plans to your partner like this.
  *At 9.00, when I arrive at work, **I'm going to** check my e-mail. Then ...*

Going to & Will

8 15.2 Complete the following conversations using the verb in brackets with either *going to* or *will*. Then listen and check your answers.

Conversation 1
A Where are you going?
B Well, I've finished everything I had to do so I (a) _____ (leave) early.
A What about the sales predictions for next month?
B Oh, I'd forgotten about that. I (b) _____ (start) on them tomorrow first thing. I've arranged to meet someone at five.

Conversation 2
C Have you planned Mr Logan's visit? What about lunch tomorrow?
D I (c) _____ (take) him to *The Redwing*.
C I seem to remember he's a vegetarian.
D Is he? In that case I (d) _____ (phone) to check they have a vegetarian menu.

Conversation 3
E Is everything confirmed for your trip to San Sebastian?
F Yes, the plane goes to Bilbao. I (e) _____ (take) the train from there.
E No, don't do that – it takes forever. The bus is much faster.
F Is it? Well, I (f) _____ (take) the bus, then.

9 Read the conversations again and look at how *will* and *going to* are used. Underline the correct option in the following sentences.

You can use *will* or *going to* to talk about decisions and plans:
  a *Will / Going to* shows that you are making a decision now.
  b *Will / Going to* shows that you made the decision earlier.

Grammar link
for more on *going to* and *will* see page 116

10 Work with a partner. Have similar conversations as in 8 using the prompts below and following this pattern:

A Say what you are **going to** do. *I'm going to walk to the station.*
B Mention a problem with the plan. *But it's raining.*
A React with an alternative plan using **will**. *Oh, in that case, I'll take a taxi.*

Plan	Problem	Alternative
walk to the station	it's raining	?
attend Japanese classes	you're too busy – you'll miss classes	?
buy a bargain computer	it's an old model – it'll be obsolete very soon	?
give up smoking	you'll get fat	?
get an easier job	you'll earn less money	?
take a taxi to the airport	the taxi drivers are on strike	?
take up roller skating	it's dangerous – there are lots of accidents	?

Wasting time

Collocations

1 Match the words to make four common collocations.

a bottom   1 balance
b delicate   2 caught
c get   3 time
d waste   4 line

2 Use the collocations in 1 to complete the article.

3 Here are the headings from the rest of the article. What tips do you think the author gives under each heading?

- Be sloppy
- The computer
- The Internet
- Office conversations
- Meetings

4 Look at page 125 to see what the author recommends.

WASTING TIME AT WORK

Lots of people are so afraid of getting caught, they never (a) _____ at work. They work the entire eight hours. They are right to be afraid. There is a (b) _____ between not doing any work and doing too much. The (c) _____ is you must get your work done. If you start wasting hours at a time, you'll (d) _____. To be an effective time waster, you have to find small ways to eat up time. Remember, you can't waste the company's time if you don't work for the company. However, with a little effort no one will ever know how little you do.

5 Complete the sentences below with words from the text on page 125 that mean the same as the words in brackets.

a 'Your papers are _____.' 'Yes, but I know where everything is so don't touch anything.' (untidy)
b Before making an important call you should _____ time to prepare it. (reserve)
c I only use the Internet to get specific information. I don't have time to _____ the web. (move around from link to link with no particular aim)
d My job requires a lot of _____ so I need a good Internet connection. (information searching)
e People who always _____ and agree with everything are no use at all. (move head up and down)

6 Work with a partner. What other ways can you think of wasting time?

Conversation skills

16 Getting things done

> The president spends most of his time kissing people on the cheek in order to get them to do what they ought to do without getting kissed.
> Harry S Truman (1884–1972), US statesman

Asking favours

1 🎧 **16.1** Complete the extracts from two conversations below which take place in an office. Then listen and compare your answers.

Extract 1

A I _____ go to the Post Office to pick something up and it's _____ . _____ lend me your umbrella?

B Of course. As long as _____ .

Extract 2

A The thing is that I need _____ where we won't be interrupted. _____ use your office?

B All right, as long as _____ . I've got a meeting myself.

What's the difference between *Could I ...?* and *Could you ...?* _____
_____

2 Work with a partner. Act out conversations using the prompts below. Use the conversations in 1 as a model.

Problem	Request	As long as ...
phone home / mobile batteries flat	use / your mobile	just a short call
send an e-mail / computer not working	use / computer	not take too long
be at airport at five / taxi services not answering	give / lift	get back before six
post a letter / can't leave the office	post it on your way home	have it ready by five o'clock
translate this letter / no dictionary	borrow yours	get it back by this afternoon
take notes / no pen	lend me one	give it back later
make copies / photocopier not working	take / photocopy shop	answer the phone while I'm out

Saying 'no'

3 🎧 **16.2** It is important to say 'no' to a request tactfully. Otherwise you can create problems for the future. Listen to the conversation and answer the questions.

a What favour does the speaker ask Richard? _____

b How does Richard react? _____

c How do you feel about lending things to people?

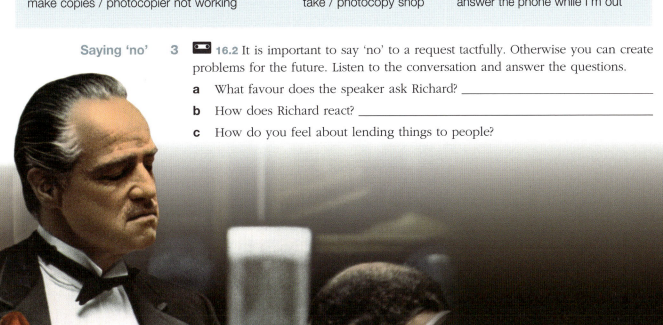

4   Use the phrases in the box to complete the conversation so that it sounds more polite.

> I'd take my own, of course, but it's being repaired.   Nothing serious, I hope.
> What's the problem?   Well, actually, I'm not very keen on the idea.
> It's just that I don't feel happy about other people driving my car.
> Oh, all right. Not to worry.

A Richard, I wonder if I could ask you a favour?
B _____
A I've got to go over to the warehouse to do something, and I haven't got my car. Would you lend me yours?
B _____
A _____
B _____
A _____
B _____
A It's just a minor scratch. Oh, don't worry. I'll think of something else.

Requests, persuasion and threats

5   🔊 16.3 Put the conversation in the correct order. Then listen and check your answer.

Jeff

☐ a   ... but on the other hand, if you do it, I'll see it as a personal favour.
☐ b   I know, but you can take the time later on.
☐ c   No, there isn't. Look, I know it's inconvenient, but I can't think of any other solution.
[1] d   Sandra, we need someone to answer the phone from 2.00 til 4.00 while Julia is off sick. Could you do it?
☐ e   Yes, in principle, yes. But you never know. Your contract is up for renewal next month. Enough said?
☐ f   No, it isn't, and obviously I can't force you to do it, but ...
☐ g   Not really. It creates such a bad impression. Listen, I'd do it myself but I've got to be somewhere else.

Sandra

☐ h   From 2.00 to 4.00? It's not my hours.
☐ i   Can't we just put the answer phone on for a couple of hours?
☐ j   Yeah, enough said.
[4] k   It's not the time. I'll have to get someone to pick the kids up from school. Isn't there anyone else?
☐ l   I see. I don't really have much choice, do I? I hope it's just this time ...
☐ m   But?
☐ n   I'm sure you would, but it's not my problem, is it?

6   Identify phrases in 5 for the following:

a   a request _____
b   a suggestion _____
c   emotional blackmail _____
d   a threat _____

Upgrade

1 🔊 **16.4**

Conversation 1 A passenger is checking in for a flight. Listen to the conversation and answer the questions.

- A Good afternoon, sir.
- B Hello. I'm on flight IB 603. I was wondering if there's any chance of an upgrade to business class.
- A Well, I don't know. It depends how crowded the flight is.
- B Yes, I quite understand, but I'd really appreciate it if you could have a look. I don't mind paying the extra. It's just that I've had a really hard day and it'd be really nice to have a bit more space and comfort.
- A Just a minute, sir.
- B I'm sorry to put you to any trouble.
- A No, that's okay. Oh, yes, there's lots of space in business class. I think we can do it.
- B Oh, fantastic. How much is that?
- A That's all right, sir. Don't worry.
- B Oh, thank you ever so much.
- A You're welcome. Have a good flight.

a What is an upgrade? _____

b Do you think the passenger really expects to pay for the upgrade? _____

c Is the passenger polite? _____

d Does he get what he wants? _____

e Underline the phrases in the conversation which the passenger uses to sound polite.

Conversation 2 A guest is checking in to a hotel. Listen to the conversation and answer the questions.

- A Good evening, sir.
- B Look, I'm not at all happy with the room you've given me. It's on the wrong side of the hotel. It faces on to the road and it's far too noisy.
- A I'm sorry, sir. No one has ever said anything before.
- B I can't believe that. Are you going to change it?
- A I don't think I can, sir. We're a bit full tonight.
- B Look, I'm really tired, and the last thing I want to do is argue about my room. If you don't change it, I'll tell my company not to use this hotel again.
- A I'm sorry. There's no other room available.
- B Oh, come on.
- A There's nothing I can do.
- B What about some sort of discount, then?
- A I'm afraid I'm not authorised to offer a discount on your room.
- B So, I have to pay the full price for a noisy room. Brilliant!
- A Sir, if you want, I can call you a taxi ...

a Do you think the guest's request is reasonable? _____

b Is the guest polite? _____

c Does he get what he wants? _____

d What other reasons can you think of for wanting to change your room?

2 Work with a partner. Act out conversation 2. This time the guest is polite. Use the phrases you underlined in conversation 1. If you are the receptionist, decide what to do.

Work issues

17 Office gossip

No one gossips about other people's secret virtues. *Bertrand Russell, British philosopher*

1 17.1 Listen to the conversation and answer the questions.

   a Why has Trixy been out of the office?
   _____

   b What is the news which she hasn't heard?
   _____

   c Is Prescott their boss or a colleague?
   _____

   d Why are they worried?
   _____

   e Why don't they think that Maureen will be worried?
   _____

   f The expression 'There's no smoke without fire' means that when people gossip about something, there's usually some truth in what they say. Do you have an equivalent saying in your language? Do you think it's true?

Reported speech

2 Look at this sentence from the conversation in 1.
... he said that we were overstaffed.
The original statement was 'You are overstaffed.'

Listen to the conversation again and complete the reported statements.

   a You will have to let some people go.
   This consultant chap _____ have to let some people go.

   b How many people does it involve?
   Prescott _____ it involved.

   c It depends on individual performance and attitude.
   He _____ on individual performance and attitude.

   d I often see them coming out of *The Green Man* together.
   I'm not saying who, but someone _____ them in The Green Man *together.*

   e Will you stay behind to work on something with me?
   The other day he _____ stay behind to work on something together.

Grammar link
for more on reported speech see page 118

Say and tell

3 Which of the sentences below needs *said* and which one needs *told?*

   a He _____ we were overstaffed.

   b He _____ me we were overstaffed.

   What is the main difference between *say* and *tell?* _____
   _____

Question words

4 What words are missing from the following sentences?

   a 'Where are you going?' He asked me _____ I was going.

   b 'When are you going?' He asked me _____ I was going.

c 'Are you going?' He asked me _____ I was going.

When reporting questions, when do you use the word *if*? _____
_____

Tenses **5** Complete the sentences below.

a 'I'm busy.' He said he _____ busy.

b 'I'll start straight away.' He said he _____ straight away.

c What changes do you make to the Present Simple in reported speech?
_____

d What changes do you make to *will* in reported speech?
_____

6 🔊 **17.2** Look at the conversations below. Complete them with words and phrases which make sense. Then listen and compare your answers.

Conversation 1

A Jeff, _____ last month's production figures?

B No, Jane, I'm _____. Can I give them to you this afternoon?

A It's no good being sorry. There's always some _____. If they're not on my desk by 4 o'clock, I'll have to _____ Mr Bradley.

B Yes, Jane. I'll start _____.

Conversation 2

C David, have you got _____? There's something I want to _____ with you ... in my office.

D What's it about?

C Oh, well, we're missing a laptop _____ from the store.

D What has that got to do with me?

C Well, you are the only other person with a _____ to the store and ...

Conversation 3

E Marie, the figures you need are _____.

F Thanks, Pedro. Is everything _____?

E Yes, no problems. Would you like to _____ them with me?

F Yes, but I'm a bit _____ this afternoon.

E Me too. Er, do _____ that new café they've just opened? It's nice and _____. We can go through them there after _____.

F Oh, I _____ so, but I won't be able to stay for long.

E Great. _____ there at about six, then?

F Yes, all right. See you there.

Conversation 4

G Hi, Monica.
H Oh, hello, Jim. _____ things going?
G Great. In fact, you can be the first to congratulate me.
H Yes, you look very _____ with yourself. What's up?
G I'm the new _____ of the eastern sales team.
H Oh, really? What salary are you on now, then?
G _____ a year.
H I can't believe it. Sixty thousand!
G And they're giving me a new _____.
H Oh, really? Congratulations, then. The _____ are on you. See you later.
G Yes. Bye.

Lexis link

for more on the vocabulary of relationships at work see page 119

7 You are at the coffee machine having a gossip with a colleague. You have overheard the conversations in 6. Use the frameworks in the box to tell your partner what you heard. It is not necessary to report everything.

| I heard ... talking to ...   ... said that ...   ... told ... that ...   ... asked ... |

Gossip

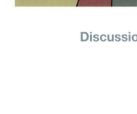

1 Read the following news article.

a What is the new law? _____

b Do you think it's a good idea? Why/why not?

City Council gags workers

Municipal employees in the Brazilian city of Cascavel have been banned from gossiping during working hours. Under a new law approved by the city council, public employees who spread rumours or gossip about their colleagues face the sack. The city says civil servants have the right to work in a professional environment and claim the new law will promote integrity in public offices.

2 Find words and phrases in the text which mean the following:

a ordered not to do something _____

b pass on information which is not official and may not be true
   _____

c be in a position where you can be dismissed _____

Discussion

3 Discuss the following with other people in the class.

a How do you define gossip?
b Is it always a bad thing?
c Is it possible to ban it?
d Does your company have a policy on gossip? Have you ever heard of a company that does?

4 The e-mails below were sent to a website for office workers. Read them and classify them in the table. Then compare your answers with a partner.

Gossip is good	Mixed feelings	Gossip is bad

A A friendly and chatty work environment makes employees happy. This results in a better level of work from employees, which means the company makes more money. Any employer who bans office gossip will lose money by making the workforce less productive.
James Pittman, England

B In my place of work gossip is the only way of finding anything out about the company strategy. The management refuse to talk to most of the staff.
Janet Jones, Wales

C There's nothing worse than gossip – and it's mostly propagated by women who have nothing better to do than YAP YAP YAP.
Luke McCarthy, Australia

D Gossip isn't a bad thing. Is there another way to learn about office politics? I see it as a healthy activity and part of working in an office.
Nicole Martin, France

E Gossip is what someone, somewhere, doesn't want you to know. A delicious pastime – unless you are the one being gossiped about. And certainly not a sackable offence.
Pieter Groot, Netherlands

F Having started a new job a year ago, I made an effort never to engage in gossip. If I'm in a group where gossip starts, I find a reason to leave the area. It can be very damaging to your career and general workplace relations.
Sanjay Patel, India

G Isn't freedom of speech a basic human right? However, there's a fine line between harmless and hurtful remarks. I think it's best left to individuals to decide which is which.
Claudia Weber, Germany

H Some of my biggest insights into problems at work have occurred while chatting by the coffee machine. Having a (brief) chat about totally unrelated matters, although not directly productive, can actually improve productivity by breaking up the day a little.
John Mason, Scotland

5 The phrases below are from the e-mails above. Complete the sentences with your own words and ideas.

a In my place of work _____

b Any employer who _____ will
_____

c There's nothing worse than _____

d _____ isn't a bad thing.

e I make an effort never to _____

f A _____ work environment makes employees
_____

6 You are going to listen to an interview about office gossip from a radio programme. The words and phrases on the left are from the interview. Match them to the definitions on the right.

a	drive for efficiency	1	talking informally
b	scrapped	2	mobile refreshments service
c	human resources	3	effort to get more work done
d	encouraged	4	seen as positive
e	chatting	5	not continued with
f	tea trolley	6	organisation and management of company staff

a	b	c	d	e	f

7 Before you listen, decide if you agree with the following statements.

a Companies who provide an opportunity for their workers to socialise are making a mistake.

b People have less time to talk to each other and socialise than before.

c The differences between a good job and a bad job are the social aspects.

d Employees are more productive when they are happy.

e When employees share information and knowledge, the company benefits.

f Companies should take measures to encourage gossip.

8 17.3 Listen to the interview to see if the speaker agrees with you.

Roleplay

9 Work with a partner and perform the following roleplay about office policy on coffee breaks and gossiping. Speaker A read the instructions below. Speaker B look at the instructions on page 133.

Speaker A

You are one of the management consultants who prepared the study mentioned in the interview in 8. In a client's company you see the notice below next to the coffee machine. Try to persuade the client to change the policy.

COMPANY NOTICE

Employees may take up to three coffee breaks per day.
Maximum time at coffee machine: four minutes.
All 'gossip' or discussion of non-work related matters is prohibited.

Writing

10 Complete the memo below.

From: Personnel Manager
To: Managing Director

With regard to the company policy on coffee breaks, _____
_____

In my opinion, _____

According to a report by the Industrial Society, _____
_____

In the report the author says that _____

It is a question of balance, but _____

In conclusion, _____

Connecting

18 E-commerce

Everyone lives by selling something. *Robert Louis Stevenson*

1 Complete the sentences using the phrases in the box. Then compare them with those on page 125. Do you agree?

> you're interested in quality   who cares?   you're interested in price
> you're interested in quality and price

a   When you buy something for yourself with your own money,
    _____

b   When you buy something for someone else with your own money,
    _____

c   When you buy something for yourself with someone else's money,
    _____

d   When you buy something for someone else with someone else's money,
    _____

Discussion 2 Work with a partner. Ask each other the following questions.

a   When was the last time you bought something for:
    - yourself?
    - somebody else?
    - a customer or client?
    - your company?

b   What did you buy?

c   What factors influenced your decisions?

d   What kind of shopping do you like/dislike?

e   Have you ever bought anything on the Internet?

focus group noun [C] a small group of people who are interviewed together and give their opinions about particular subjects, usually to help a company or political party make decisions

from *Macmillan English Dictionary*

3 You are going to listen to a focus group discussion from the radio programme *Marketing Today*. The topic is marketing to teenagers on the Internet. Before you listen, look at the headings on the notepad below. What do you think the participants will say about the different topics?

Teenagers and Internet marketing

Opportunities
　Attitude to technology and the Internet:
　_____

　Financial responsibilities and spending power:
　_____

Problems
　Differences between teenage age groups:
　_____

　Main uses teenagers make of the Internet:
　_____

　Main problem teenagers have when they buy online:
　_____

　Morality of marketing to teenagers:
　_____

Possible solution – 'Splash Plastic'
　What is it?
　_____

　How it works:
　_____

　What products teenagers can buy with it:
　_____

---

4 **18.1** Listen to the focus group discussion between the host and three marketing experts. Complete the notes in 3.

5 You are preparing a report on using the Internet to market to teenagers. Use your notes in 3 to complete the introduction to the report.

TEENAGERS AND THE INTERNET

TEENAGERS are an opportunity for companies marketing over the Internet for two reasons. Firstly, their attitude to new technology is generally _____. Secondly, unlike adults, they have no _____.

However, marketing to this age group presents special problems. One problem is age. The average age
5　of the heaviest users is _____, but they want to buy things aimed at _____. Another is that they don't want to ask _____. As a result, they tend to use the Internet for communication, but _____. One possible solution is the Splash Plastic magnetic swipe card. Kids can top it up with cash at selected stores, and then use it to _____. This avoids problems with the parents because _____.
10　However, for some people there is also a _____ in marketing to teenagers who will buy things in an impulsive and irresponsible way.

In conclusion, in spite of the problems, for e-commerce to be a success in the future, we have to take advantage of the fact that _____.

6 Listen again and complete the sentences. There is a space for each missing word. Contractions count as one word.

a According to their parents, teenagers wear too much make-up, treat the house like a hotel and run up huge phone bills. _____ _____ _____ _____, for e-commerce teenagers are a dream.

b Lucy, you're the marketing manager of one of these teen sites – Wicked Colours. _____ _____ _____ _____ the future of e-commerce in this market?

c _____ _____ _____ _____ _____ is age. Some sites try to target an age group that's too wide.

d Yes, _____ _____ _____ _____ _____ _____ all 13-year-olds want to be 18-year-olds.

e _____ _____, and that's why, in my opinion, the teenager market has no future.

f I think Brian will _____ _____ _____ _____ _____ .

g Actually, _____ _____ _____, Nick.

h Well, _____ _____ _____ _____, but rightly or wrongly, the current generation of teenagers will have an important influence on the future of e-commerce.

7 Look at this phrase from the discussion.

*The right audience **is one thing, but** getting them to buy directly from your site **is another**.*

Make similar sentences using the following prompts.

a the right qualifications / have experience

<u>The right qualifications for a job are one thing, but having experience is another.</u>

b a high turnover / make good profits

_____

c have a good idea / put into practice

_____

d high productivity / improve staff motivation

_____

e create a good product / sell it

_____

📼 **18.2** Now listen and compare your answers.

8 Make three examples relating to your job using the same structure as in 7.

Discussion

9 Discuss the following questions.
  a What makes teenagers want to buy things?
  b What products do they buy?
  c How do you sell them things?
  d In your opinion, is it ethical to target teenage consumers as a market? Should there be government limitations? If so, what should they be?

Roleplay

10 Work in groups of three. You all work for a marketing company. Market studies have shown that retired people spend a significant amount of their free time surfing the Internet. You have formed a focus group to explore the possibility of marketing to the over-sixties using the Internet. Make notes about what you are going to say. Use some of the expressions in 6 and 7 in your discussion.

Speaker A You think this is a fantastic idea. Think of arguments to support it.

Speaker B You think this is a ridiculous idea. Think of arguments against it.

Speaker C You are the focus group leader. You are not sure about this idea. Lead the discussion, listen to the others and ask questions.

The future of e-commerce

Vocabulary

1 The words and phrases a–h are from an article on the future of e-commerce. Match them to the explanations 1–8.

  a to comparison shop
  b catalogue shopping
  c voice recognition
  d a keyboard
  e a range of options
  f historical preferences
  g to virtually shop
  h to try on

  1 to compare the products offered by different suppliers
  2 the thing you use to type text into a computer
  3 to see if clothes fit you and suit you
  4 to buy things online
  5 information based on past customer choices
  6 a system where customers buy by post
  7 a number of different choices
  8 a system where a computer understands spoken instructions

a	b	c	d	e	f	g	h

2 Match the headings below to the paragraphs in the article on page 85. There is one heading you don't need. Write the correct heading number in each box.

  1 What consumers really want
  2 'Real' e-commerce
  3 Consumers want more than just convenience
  4 Why e-commerce isn't working
  5 The virtual shopping assistant
  6 Goodbye to the keyboard

SHOPPING FROM HOME

What forms of e-commerce will dominate the next millennium? What is it that the consumer really wants and will pay for? For a while, companies believed that consumers wanted convenience more than the best price. Catalogue shopping works on this principle, but it makes up only two per cent of the economy.

Consumers really want things to be simple, easy and fast. They want to be entertained when they shop. They want to comparison shop. They want the best service. They want great prices. The Internet and e-commerce can provide all of this.

High definition graphics and video will be part of the everyday online shopping experience. People will be able to virtually shop and interact with their friends without leaving home. Artificial intelligence will put a virtual shop assistant at the service of every online shopper. She will suggest colours, sizes and other features that match the shopper's preferences. These will be stored on the company's computers.

The biggest obstacle to the Net is the keyboard. Voice recognition will make it obsolete. The consumer will access the network from anywhere – from home, the car, or perhaps even from a pair of glasses.

The consumer will say, 'I'd like to buy a red sweater today, something in the $25 to $30 range.' The network will take that request, along with any other historical preferences the consumer has – such as size, style and fabric. It will assemble a range of options at different prices from a variety of stores. All in the consumer's exact size. Then the consumer will be able to virtually try on the different sweaters using a 3D model of herself stored in the computer. And that is real e-commerce.

3 Complete the sentences below with the vocabulary items in 1. Each sentence expresses an opinion. Do you agree?

a They should completely redesign the computer _____. It's uncomfortable and badly organised.

b I would never buy a suit online. I love going to shops and having the opportunity _____ clothes and feel the quality of the material.

c _____ may be popular in the USA but nobody buys things that way in my country.

d I don't like the idea of _____. I feel silly talking to a machine and it probably wouldn't understand me well.

e I never have time _____. If I see something I like, I usually buy it on impulse.

f I think I will always prefer to go to a high street clothes store than _____.

g I like shopping in big shopping centres because they offer _____ that small shops can't compete with.

h I object to the way some websites leave 'cookies' on your computer which record your _____ from previous visits.

> **Lexis link**
>
> for more on the vocabulary of shopping and the Internet see page 121

Making predictions

1 Look at this sentence from the article on page 85.

*The consumer **will access** the network from anywhere.*

This is a prediction. You express predictions about the future using **will**. Underline other predictions in the article.

2 Do you agree with the predictions in the article? Discuss them like this:

A **I think** DVD **will replace** the cinema.
B Do you? I don't. / Me too.
A **I don't think** the keyboard **will become** obsolete.
B Don't you? I do. / Me neither.

> **Grammar link**
>
> for more on *will* for future predictions see page 120

3 What other predictions can you make about the Internet? For example:

*In ten years all banking **will be** online.*

Discussion

4 Tick Y (yes) or N (no) against the predictions in the chart so that they are true for you. Then discuss them with a partner. For example:

A Do you think you'll change your job in the next five years?
B Yes, I do. I don't really like what I do now. How about you?
A No, I don't think I will. Things are going well and I like my job.

	next year	Y N	in five years	Y N	in the next ten years	Y N
my life	I'll change jobs.	☐ ☐	I'll leave and start my own company.	☐ ☐	I'll make a million and retire.	☐ ☐
my company	Our main competitor will go bankrupt.	☐ ☐	Everybody will work at home most of the time.	☐ ☐	Most employees will be replaced by computers.	☐ ☐
the world	There will be an economic boom.	☐ ☐	The USA will have a black president.	☐ ☐	There'll be a world government.	☐ ☐

Work issues

19 Working from home

Mid pleasures and palaces though we may roam,
Be it ever so humble, there's no place like home;
Home, home, sweet, sweet home!
There's no place like home! There's no place like home!
John Howard Payne, US actor and dramatist

1 Read the news item below and discuss the questions with a partner.

GO HOME AND WORK

A major international telecommunications company wants to persuade 10,000 of its employees to work from home. They believe that if the staff used computers, fax machines, mobile phones and the Internet, they would maintain the same levels of productivity as when they work in the office. In their talks with the unions, the company argues that amongst other advantages, the plan will make it possible to:

- close down office buildings and save on expensive city centre rents
- demonstrate the effectiveness of its telecommunications equipment
- reduce investment in new offices and office improvements
- improve the quality of life for workers
- help preserve the environment by reducing home to office travel

a What do you think of the company's arguments in favour of the plan?
b What is the most important reason for the proposal?
c How would you feel about the plan if you worked for this company?

Conditionals (future reference)

2 Look at question c in 1 again. Answer it using the words below.

If I worked for this company, _____
I'd be happy if _____
I wouldn't be happy if _____

3 You use *if* + past + *would/could* to talk about hypothetical or imagined situations. Underline another example of this structure in the news item in 1.

4 A company manager is sitting in his office dreaming about how he could change his life. Put his ideas into a chain of conditionals to recreate his dream like this:

If I left my job, I'd spend more time at home.   If I spent more time at home, ...

> have time to think   come up with a really great business idea
> have a lot of responsibilities   be completely stressed out again
> set up a company   be more relaxed
> have to work harder than I want to   be an enormous success

Grammar link

for more on conditionals (future reference) see page 122

teleworker /ˈteliˌwɜːkə/ noun [C] someone who works at home on a computer and communicates with their office or customers by telephone, fax, or email

from *Macmillan English Dictionary*

5 In what circumstances would you …
- work from home?
- stop working altogether?
- change jobs?
- refuse a promotion?
- ask for a pay rise?
- accept a cut in pay?

For example: *I'd work from home if my company offered us the opportunity.*

Teleworking

1 19.1 Listen to two interviews with people who telework. Which speaker:

a has children? _____
b lives in the country? _____
c doesn't have fixed hours? _____
d gets up later than before? _____
e wears her slippers to work? _____
f is self employed? _____
g works for a company? _____

2 Listen again and complete the chart.

	Speaker 1	Speaker 2
Country		
What did she do before?		
What does she do now?		
What are the advantages of her new work?		
What are the advantages for her employers/clients?		

Discussion

3 Which of the speakers is making a better use of technology, in your opinion? What would the main advantages and disadvantages of working from home be for you?

4 Read the advantages and disadvantages of working from home in the magazine article on page 89. Put each in the correct category in the chart below. The first one has been done for you.

Does working at home really work?	Advantages	Disadvantages
The workplace		
The working day		
Commuting		
Technology		
Efficiency		
Costs		
Motivation		
Family		✓

WORKING AT HOME
THE ADVANTAGES AND DISADVANTAGES

What do people *really* think about working from home? We interviewed a cross section of people from different industries about their experiences of teleworking. As you will see, there was quite a wide variety of opinions.

1 'There is no getting away from the family. When you work in an office you get a chance to escape and meet new people.'

2 'I think us home workers get more done in a shorter time. There are no phone calls or colleagues to slow you down.'

3 'Without the journeys to and from the office you don't get a chance to relax and prepare your mind before you work, or to wind down before you get home. I miss the separation between home and leisure time.'

4 'You *do* get to see more of your children. The problem is, though, that you're supposed to be WORKING.'

5 'You don't have to sit in traffic jams or walk to work in the rain. Or listen to people talking loudly on their mobiles on the train.'

6 'I think financially you miss out on perks like subsidised refreshments or travel.'

7 'Life is definitely cheaper for the employee. You save on things like transport and smart clothes. It's also cheaper to have lunch at home.'

8 'It's a bit dangerous for workaholics. You can easily find your working time creeping into your leisure time.'

9 'Sharing ideas and problems with your colleagues can make you more productive in some jobs. And the gossip can be really inspiring!'

10 'Space can be a problem. Rooms can become an unpleasant mix of home and office.'

11 'You don't have to work with those obsolete office computers and the company intranet which always seems to be down.'

12 'The flexibility is great. You can work at five in the morning or on a Sunday afternoon.'

13 'I like the freedom. You can open the window, play music and generally make yourself comfortable.'

14 'It can be difficult to get down to work. You have to be very self-disciplined.'

15 'If you have a technical problem, you're on your own. There's no IT expert to call on.'

16 'No boss cracking the whip!'

5 Look at the chart on page 125 and check your answers.

Vocabulary

6 Find words and phrases in the text which mean the same as:

a relax _____

b queues of cars and lorries unable to move forward _____

c benefits not included in your salary _____

d people who can't stop working _____

e out of date and no longer useful _____

f informal exchange of news and information _____

g start _____

h trying to make people work harder _____

7 Complete the sentences with the words and phrases from 6.

a As I have to travel so much I miss out on all the office _____.

b When I get home, I like to _____ by listening to some classical music with a glass of wine.

c My boss is a complete _____. She just doesn't know how to relax and turn off.

d It's better to have a higher salary than _____ like a company car or free meals.

e The problem with buying a computer is that in a couple of years it's _____.

f I find it difficult to _____ the accounts and usually leave them until the last minute.

g I leave home very early to avoid getting caught in _____ on the way to work.

h _____ is part of any manager's job.

Lexis link

for more on the vocabulary of teleworking see page 123

8 Are the sentences in 7 true for you? If not, change them so that they are.

Roleplay

9 Work with a partner and perform the following roleplay about the advantages of working at home or in the office. Use the phrases in the box to help you.

Speaker A You are a manager in your company. You are negotiating with the unions to introduce the policies mentioned in the news item on page 87. Convince your partner of the advantages of working at home.

Speaker B You are a union representative in speaker A's company. The management wants to introduce working from home but you are against it. Convince your partner of the advantages of office work.

> If people worked from home, ...   Most people find / would find that ...
> From the worker's / company's point of view, it would mean ...
> At the moment, people have to ...   There'd be all sorts of problems if ...
> I agree with that, but ...   That's not necessarily true, because if ...

Conversation skills

20 Working lunch

Vegetables are interesting but lack a sense of purpose when unaccompanied by a good cut of meat. *Fran Lebowitz*

1   20.1 Neil Klein and Satoshi Tanaka are having a working lunch at a restaurant in Japan. Listen to their conversation and answer the questions.

   a   Why does Neil like the restaurant? _____
   b   Who orders the food? _____
   c   What does Neil want to eat? _____
   d   What does Neil decide to eat? _____

2   Put the lines of the conversation in 1 in order. Then listen again and check.

   Neil Klein
   [1] This looks like a very nice place, Satoshi.
   [ ] I'll try the *unagi*, then.
   [ ] Okay. Sounds good.
   [ ] What's that?
   [ ] Yes, I really like the decor. Er, could you order for both of us, Satoshi?
   [ ] Hm, I'm sure it is. Actually, do you think I could have a steak?
   [ ] No, no, let's have some sake.

   Satoshi Tanaka
   [ ] And then I think you should try some *unagi*.
   [ ] It's eel – grilled and served on a bed of rice. It's delicious.
   [ ] Yes, I thought you would like it.
   [ ] Well, I'm afraid they don't serve steak here.
   [ ] Fine. Would you like some sake, or would you prefer some beer?
   [ ] Of course. I think we could have some miso soup to start with. They do it very well here.
   [14] Right. Sake it is, then.

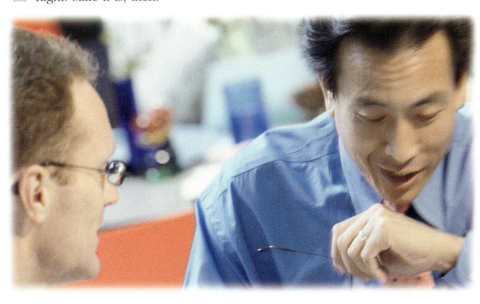

Starters
Onion bhaji
Samosa

Main courses
Chicken Madras
Vegetable Biryani

3
a Make a list of some of the typical dishes which restaurants serve in your area, using the local name.

b Imagine you are entertaining a visitor. Sometimes you can translate the names of dishes, but you may also have to explain how they are cooked. Act out a conversation with a partner and explain what each dish consists of. Use the phrases on the right to help you.

	a type of	fish meat vegetable pie
	a	rice dish pasta dish
It's	made with made from	eggs fruit
	served with	vegetables a salad potatoes a sauce
	cooked	with garlic with spices with herbs in olive oil

Who does what?

1 20.2 Complete the second part of Neil and Satoshi's conversation with the phrases in the box. Then listen and check your answers.

> job title   report to   responsible for

Satoshi Neil, I met Jeff Segram earlier this year. What exactly is his _____?

Neil He's the Managing Director.

Satoshi Do you mean the CEO?

Neil Yes, that's what the Americans say. He's the person on the board who is _____ the day to day running of the company.

Satoshi And what about you?

Neil I'm the Product Development Director. I'm on the board as well, but I _____ Jeff.

Satoshi Right, I see.

2 Find phrases in the conversation in 1 which are similar in meaning to the following:

a is in charge of _____

b Jeff is my boss. _____

c What does he do? _____

3 Act out conversations like the one in exercise 1 using the prompts below. Use your own ideas, if you like.

Who you met	Job title	Responsibilities	Your job title	Who you report to
John Atherstone	Chairman/President	long-term strategy and planning	Managing Director	John Atherstone
Sisi Albright	Director of Marketing/ Vice-President Marketing	marketing policy and the worldwide sales force	Head of Asian Sales Department	Sisi Albright

4 Work with a partner.
  a List five job titles in your company, or in other companies.
  b Do you know the equivalent job titles in English?
  c Explain what each person does.

Down to business

1 20.3 Listen to Neil Klein talking to Jeff Segram when he returned to head office, and answer the questions.

  a Was the trip a success? _____
  b What do you think happened when they got down to business?

2 20.4 Now listen to the conversation between Neil and Satoshi. What do you think Neil did wrong?

_____

_____

3 Read the information on the right about doing business in Japan. Does this confirm your ideas in 2?

4 Act out the conversation between Neil and Satoshi, but this time Neil should follow the advice in the text.

5 Do you have any similar experiences doing business with different cultures? What other differences in the way of doing business do you know about?

The Hard Sell

A hard sell is often seen as offensive in Japan. Japanese business people may think that you are trying to convince them because your product is no good. It is better to use a low-key sales pitch and give them objective information. Japanese are not accustomed to aggressive American techniques that use a persuasive 'winning' argument. If you are not completely honest about your product, your credibility will be damaged and what you say will lose influence. Don't say that yours is 'the best on the market'. It is better to say, 'We sold two million units last year. As you know, our closest competitor sold less than a million.' At the same time, be careful not to criticise competing products. In fact, the Japanese will respect you if you mention the assets of the competition.

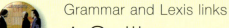

Grammar and Lexis links
1 Selling your company

Present Simple

Affirmative	
I you we they	work
he she it	works

Negative	
I you we they	don't work
he she it	doesn't work

Interrogative		
do don't	I you we they	work?
does doesn't	he she it	work?

You use the Present Simple to talk about

- routine actions and habits.
  *I **go** to work by bus.*
  *He **works** late on Tuesdays.*

- ongoing situations we see as stable.
  *We **live** in London.*
  *They **employ** over 250 people.*

Present Continuous

Affirmative	
I'm (am)	
you're (are) we're (are) they're (are)	working
he's (is) she's (is) it's (is)	

Negative	
I'm not	
you aren't we aren't they aren't	working
he isn't she isn't it isn't	

Interrogative		
am aren't	I	
are aren't	you we they	working?
is isn't	he she it	

You use the Present Continuous to talk about

- activities happening at the moment of speaking.
  *He**'s** **wearing** a grey suit, a white shirt and a blue tie.*
  *Don't interrupt me, please. I**'m trying** to concentrate.*
  *'What **are** you **doing**?' 'I**'m preparing** this month's sales figures.'*

- activities or situations you see as temporary.
  *We**'re using** this office until the new one is ready.*
  *I**'m working** from home for a few days so don't phone me at the office.*

- situations which are changing.
  *The economic situation **is getting** better.*
  *Our company share price **is** steadily **improving**.*

You often use the Present Continuous with time expressions *at the moment, this week/month/year* etc.

*We **are having** a lot of problems with our suppliers **at the moment**.*

*I**'m doing** a course **this month**, but it's not very interesting.*

Practice 1 Complete the sentences using the verbs in the box in the correct form – Present Simple or Present Continuous. Use each verb twice.

work	get	sell	do	think	live

a Normally I am in the office in the afternoon but this month I _____ a course.

b In the winter the reps _____ more than in the summer.

c Our most important market is the Far East. We _____ business with several companies there.

d Our new product line _____ very well this year.

e Our boss _____ very long hours.

f He _____ of changing his job because he's not very happy.

g 'What's your address?' 'I _____ in a hotel until we find a nice flat.'

h In June the weather _____ hot there so take some cool clothes.

i He _____ his job is really interesting.

j It _____ hotter. We need to get some air conditioning for this office.

k At present we _____ on new products and services for the future.

l During the week he _____ in his city flat and at the weekend he goes to the country.

Practice 2 Write questions about the information which is missing.

a The company makes money by ...
   How does the company make money?

b Our business is expanding because ...
   Why _____

c They are setting up a business in ...
   Where _____

d We are looking for $ ...
   How much _____

e He has previous experience in the ... business.
   What kind _____
   _____

f Their competitive advantage is ...
   What _____

g My company employs ... people.
   How many _____

h The manager of the company is ...
   Who _____

i They are talking to ... about further investment.
   Who _____

Lexis: Business & the Internet

Running a business Complete the sentences using the words in the box.

average	worth	campaigns	costs
experience	Internet	investment	turnover
employs	margin	website

a The company _____ over 2,000 workers in Europe, located in four different factories.

b Our running _____ include rent, electricity and equipment hire, as well as salaries.

c Direct mail _____ can sometimes be very effective, but it depends on the product.

d Our company _____ provides information about our services and products, but we don't sell anything online.

e We need more _____ to finance our marketing plan, so we are talking to venture capitalists in the USA.

f The _____ of 4, 6, 8 and 10 is 7.

g He has an MBA but does he have any previous _____ in this kind of business?

h For the company to survive, our _____ needs to grow by 20% this year.

i In my opinion, the BBC has one of the best websites on the _____.

j They make a profit of $4.20 on each book they sell, which represents a _____ of 60%.

k The business is _____ over $30m.

The Internet & computers Complete the crossword.

Across

2 We are designing a new _____ at the moment.
3 Please add our site to your _____ of favourites.
5 If you give me your address, I can send you an _____.
7 A _____ with no cable is much more comfortable to use.
9 It's like the Internet but the pages are only accessible inside the company.
10 We pay them to include a _____ to our website on their page.
11 How much do you pay for your Internet _____ per month?
14 Our system is infected by a _____.
16 I don't have much time to _____ the Internet at work.

Down

1 I'll send you the document as an e-mail _____.
4 Don't get so close to the _____. It's bad for your eyes.
6 You can _____ music and pictures from our site.
8 Nowadays I buy all my CDs and books _____.
12 _____ here for further information.
13 I'm looking for a web_____ with information about share prices.
15 In order to _____ the web in comfort you need a good computer.

Answers on page 124

Grammar and Lexis links
2 Women in business

Expressing frequency

To say how often something happens you use:

- Adverbs of frequency
  *always   usually   often   sometimes   not often
  hardly ever   never*

  The adverb comes *before* the main verb:

I You We They He She	(don't/doesn't) **usually** (don't/doesn't) **often** **sometimes** **never**	drive(s) to work. go(es) out for lunch.

  but *after* the verb 'to be'.

I	am		
You We They	are	(not) **usually** (not) **often** **sometimes** **never**	late. tired.
He She	is		

- Frequency expressions
  every day/week
  once/twice/three times a day/week/month/year   etc.

  These expressions come at the beginning or end of the sentence.

I You We They He She	have (has) a break go(es) on holiday	every day. once twice three times four times	a day. a week. a month. a year.

Every day		I you we they he she	have (has) a break. go(es) on holiday.
Once Twice Three times Four times	a day a week a month a year		

Practice 1 Reorganise the words and phrases to make correct sentences.

a   abroad   times   I   a   year   travel   four
_____

b   a   on   department   meeting   we   always   have   Monday   morning
_____
_____

c   often   he   to   Germany   doesn't   go
_____

d   manager   the   department   usually   leaves   on   Friday   early
_____
_____

e   I   use   the   car   never   can't   because   drive   I
_____

f   has   the   office   canteen   she   always   lunch   in
_____

g   often   they   for   work   aren't   late
_____

h   always   Microsoft   is   the   news   in
_____

i   my   every   I   change   mobile   year
_____

j   ever   do   you   have   parties   office?
_____

k   often   to   how   gym   you   the   do   go?
_____

l   you   your   do   use   much   laptop?
_____

Practice 2 Rewrite the question using question words *what, who, when* etc.

a   Do you go to work by car? On foot?
   How do you go to work?

b   Do you use the phone a lot? Ever?
_____

c   Do you get to work at 8.30? 9.00?
_____

d   Does he do the housework because he likes it? Because he has to?
_____

e   Does he play squash every day? Every week?
_____

f   Does she go to work with her husband? A friend?
_____

g   Do you spend the morning making plans? Having meetings?
_____

h Do you work 35 hours a week? Forty hours a week?

i Does it take you 20 minutes to read the newspaper? Half an hour?

j Do you work so hard because it's fun? Because you need the money?

Lexis: Work & routines

1 Match the parts of the sentences below.
   a Professor Axt thinks that lazing ...
   b Doing as little as possible is better ...
   c Lying about is the key ...
   d Take a midday break instead ...
   e He's in favour ...
   f Try to take ...
   g We only have a limited ...
   h If you get up early, you are likely to ...

   1 ... around is good for you.
   2 ... of playing squash or going for a run.
   3 ... amount of energy.
   4 ... it easy this weekend.
   5 ... than going to the gym.
   6 ... to a long life.
   7 ... of moderate exercise like walking.
   8 ... feel stressed for the rest of the day.

a	b	c	d	e	f	g	h
1							

2 Write in the missing pairs of words below.

developing + sales   engineer + degree
ratio + to   experience + qualifications
charge + hiring   productive + day
marketing + women   get + off

   a We only _____ half an hour _____ for lunch.
   b You should get some practical _____ as well as _____.
   c She's in _____ of _____ and firing.
   d Why do _____ departments have more _____ than men?
   e If you want to be an _____, you'll need a _____.
   f The _____ of men to women is two _____ one in my job.

g Nobody can be _____ sixteen hours a _____.

h She's involved in _____ new _____ strategies.

***Do* as an auxiliary** Complete the conversation using *do, does, don't* or *doesn't*.

A (a) _____ you do a lot of exercise?
B Yes, I suppose I (b) _____. Why do you ask?
A Well, it's better if you (c) _____, according to a German scientist.
B What (d) _____ he say about it?
A He (e) _____ say that exercise is bad for you exactly, but that if you do too much, you use up all your energy.
B That (f) _____ make sense. Sport is good for you and makes you feel better.
A Yes, but according to him people who run marathons and play squash (g) _____ usually live to an old age.
B Well, I (h) _____ believe it. He probably just (i) _____ like sport.

Jobs Reorganise the letters to form words related to jobs. Then complete the sentences using the words.

soipoint   driteer   litte   texecuvie   nacharim
contacaunt   nagream   denistrep

   a She's the chief _____ officer.
   b He's the _____ of the board.
   c He doesn't work, he's _____.
   d The CEO is the top _____ in the company.
   e Her job _____ is 'vice president'.
   f It's hard to explain what I do, but I guess I'm a sort of _____.
   g The financial director of the company is a qualified _____.
   h The job title '_____' sounds more important than 'chairman'.

Grammar and Lexis links
3 Telephone talk

Indirect questions

Direct questions	Indirect questions	Differences
Where **are you** from?	Can you tell me **where you are** from?	• Word order
How **is she**?	**how she is**?	• No *do* or *does*
Where **are we** meeting?	Can you remember where **we're** meeting?	• *if* in Yes/No questions
Where **do you live**?	Could you tell me **where you live**?	
How much money **does he earn**?	**how much money he earns**?	
Does he like football?	Do you know **if he likes** football	
Has he got my address?	**if he has got** my address?	

Practice 1 Reorganise the words to make indirect questions or statements.

a   tell if got my me could you she message
_____

b   know be back will do when he you
_____

c   do long know takes you how it
_____

d   remember the what bus time can leaves you
_____

e   this know do what word you means
_____

f   know think he wants what you to do
_____

g   idea the is time I've no what
_____

Practice 2 Change the direct questions into indirect questions.

a   What time does the meeting begin?
Do you know _____

b   How much is the hotel?
Could you tell me _____

c   Why is he angry?
Do you know _____

d   Is there a restaurant car on the train?
Can you tell me _____

e   Where can I park the car?
Can you tell me _____

f   Is the office near the town centre?
Can you remember _____

Lexis: On the telephone

Numbers Write the full form of the numbers and figures.

a   321   *three hundred and twenty-one*
b   69%   _____
c   3,428   _____
d   6.392   _____
e   £3m   _____
f $9.39   _____
g   24,678,902   _____

Telephone phrases

1   Put the conversation below in the correct order.

☐   Hello, ADH Graphics.

☐   Yes, please. Could you ask him to phone John Clarkson from Bellstone & Smith? He has the phone number.

☐   Just one moment ... I'm sorry, there's no answer.

☐   Yes, of course. Could I just check your name? John Clark from Bellstone & Smith.

☐   Thank you. Goodbye.

☐   Oh, dear. I'm phoning for some information. It's quite urgent. Do you know where I can contact him?

☐   Oh, good morning. Could I speak to Peter White, please?

☐   No, sorry, I'm afraid I don't. Can I take a message?

☐   No, it's Clarkson. He knows what it's about.

☐   Oh, sorry, Mr Clarkson. I'll tell him as soon as he's available.

2 Complete the conversation using the words and phrases in the box.

> Could I speak to   hold   put me through
> Can I take a message?   call me   bad line
> This is   engaged   You're through
> dialled the wrong number

A   Sales Department. Can I help you?

B   Oh! I must have

(a) _____. Can you

(b) _____ to Customer

Services, please?

A   I'm sorry, it's a (c) _____.
Did you say Customer Services?

B   Yes, that's right.

A   Just one moment. I'm sorry, but the line is

(d) _____. Do you want to

(e) _____?

B   All right.

A   (f) _____ now.

B   Hello. (g) _____ the
department manager, please?

C   I'm afraid he's not in the office this morning.

(h) _____?

B   Yes, please. (i) _____ George
Smith. Could you ask him to

(j) _____?

C   Yes, of course. Goodbye.

B   Bye.

3 Match the parts of the sentences below.

a   Tell her it's Mr Jenkins. I'm returning ...
b   Typical! I got cut ...
c   I hate it when they put you ...
d   I keep getting an engaged ...
e   Could you say ...
f   Can you read that ...

1   ... on hold, and then forget about you.
2   ... back to me, just to check?
3   ... tone. Maybe his phone is off the hook.
4   ... her call this morning.
5   ... that again, please? I didn't understand.
6   ... off in the middle of the call.

a	b	c	d	e	f
4					

4 Match the words to their definitions.

☐ **a** telephone directory   ☐ **g** wrong number
☐ **b** engaged   ☐ **h** switchboard
☑ **c** dialling tone   ☐ **i** extension number
☐ **d** reverse charge call   ☐ **j** cell phone
☐ **e** national call   ☐ **k** directory enquiries
☐ **f** off-peak call   ☐ **l** operator

1   A continuous sound that means you can dial the number you want.
2   The equipment which distributes calls to the different departments and offices in a company.
3   A phone number you dial by mistake.
4   Busy – someone is using the line you want.
5   The number of each different phone in a company.
6   A call which is paid for by the person you are calling.
7   Also called a mobile phone.
8   A book with a list of telephone numbers.
9   A service you phone if you want to find a number.
10   A call to a different part of the country.
11   A person who helps you make a call.
12   A call made in the evening or at the weekend which has a lower charge.

5 Rewrite the following conversation to make it sound more polite.

Galaxy Computers Galaxy Computers. What do you want?

a   *Galaxy Computers. Can I help you?*

Michael Jones I want to speak to Harris.

b   _____

Galaxy Computers Who are you?

c   _____

Michael Jones Jones. ABC Industries.

d   _____
_____

Galaxy Computers Who? What's your name again?

e   _____
_____

Michael Jones Michael Jones.

Galaxy Computers He's speaking to someone on his line. Want to wait?

f   _____
_____

Michael Jones No. Tell him I called, right?

g   _____

Galaxy Computers No problem. Bye.

h   _____

Grammar and Lexis links

5 Company histories

Past Simple

Affirmative	
I you he she it we they	worked

Negative	
I you he she it we they	didn't work

Interrogative		
did didn't	I you he she it we they	work?

Formation: regular verbs

infinitive
- work – work**ed**

infinitive ending in e
- like – lik**ed**

infinitive ending in consonant + y
- hurry – hurr**ied**

one syllable verbs ending in one vowel + one consonant
- stop – stop**ped**

   (except verbs ending in w or y)
- play – play**ed**, show – show**ed**

two syllable verbs with the stress on the second syllable
- prefER – prefer**red**, admIT – admit**ted**

two syllable words with the stress on the first syllable
- VISit – visit**ed**, ENter – enter**ed**

Formation: irregular verbs
Many of the most common verbs are irregular.
go – **went**, come – **came**

You use the Past Simple to express finished actions, events or situations.
We **moved** to a new office last year.*
Before I got married I **lived** in Lisbon.
In my first job, I **travelled** a lot.

*You often use the Past Simple with expressions describing completed periods of time: *three weeks ago, last year, on Tuesday, in March, at Christmas*, etc.

Time expressions
To say *when* things happen in the past, you use:
- in + month / year – *in March, in 1987*
- on + day / date – *on Monday, on 5th December*
- at + time / special periods – *at 5.00, at Christmas*
- length of time + ago – *five minutes ago, a week ago*
- when + past situation / action – *when I was younger, when he arrived*

Practice 1 Write the Past Simple of the verbs below.

work <u>worked</u>   marry _____
stop <u>stopped</u>   plan _____
live _____   reach _____
start _____   arrive _____
use _____   fit _____
travel _____   visit _____
drop _____   call _____
carry _____   increase _____
tip _____   like _____

Practice 2 The twelve verbs below are some of the most common in English. They are all irregular. Write the Past Simple of each.

tell _____   make _____
say _____   do _____
get _____   go _____
give _____   come _____
take _____   write _____
put _____   have _____

Practice 3 Complete the sentences with one of the words in the box or put 'X' when no word is necessary.

| ago in for at when on |

a John started working here _____ Christmas and he spoke to me for the first time ten minutes _____.
b I travelled a lot _____ last year.
c _____ Monday I had a meeting with Mr Leblanc.
d I sent them the fax _____ Monday.
e _____ I lived in London, I usually went away _____ the weekend.
f The delegation from Geneva arrived _____ three o'clock.
g I worked for IBM _____ three years.
h We had a really interesting business trip to Turkey _____ March.
i I had a meeting _____ 9.30 _____ the evening and eventually got to my hotel _____ two _____ the morning.

100   5 Grammar and Lexis link

j When I woke up _____ yesterday morning, I didn't know where I was.

k Did Mr Heinkers phone _____ I was out?

Practice 4 The following facts are incorrect. Make the sentences negative. Then give the correct information.

a Bill Gates founded Oracle.
   Bill Gates didn't found Oracle, he founded Microsoft.

b On October 4 1929 the Wall Street Crash started a worldwide economic boom.
   _____
   _____

c On March 25 1957 six European states signed the Treaty of Madrid, creating the EEC.
   _____
   _____

d On January 1 1999 eleven member states of the European Union adopted the pound as a common currency.
   _____
   _____

e Henry Ford manufactured the first mass produced electronic components.
   _____
   _____

f In 2001 Napster had legal problems over people downloading books.
   _____
   _____

Answers on page 127

Practice 5 Write questions about the missing information.

a I went to ____ on my last business trip.
   Where did you go on your last business trip?

b He set up the company in ____.
   When _____

c They started selling ____ last year.
   _____

d At first the product sold well because ____.
   _____

e They made a profit by ____.
   _____

f He worked for ICI for ____ years.
   _____

g I spoke to ____ at the conference.
   _____

h ____ invented the mobile phone.
   _____

i ____ people work in the Lille factory.
   _____

j I travelled from Munich to Berlin by ____.
   _____

Practice 6 Complete the article using the verbs in the box in the Past Simple.

be convert develop begin be grow become

Like many other aspects of the computer age, *Yahoo!* started as an idea, (1) _____ into a hobby and then (2) _____ a full-time passion. The two developers of *Yahoo!*, David Filo and Jerry Yang, (3) _____ Ph.D. students in electrical engineering at Stanford University when they (4) _____ working on *Yahoo!* in April 1994. At first it (5) _____ a way to keep track of their personal interests on the Internet. Later they (6) _____ their personal lists into a database designed to serve the needs of any user. They (7) _____ software to help them locate, identify and edit material stored on the Internet. Today, *Yahoo!* contains organised information on tens of thousands of computers linked to the Web.

Lexis: Business verbs

Complete the sentences below with an appropriate verb.

a His ambition is to _____ the president of the company.

b The company plans to _____ a new product line.

c To make money companies need to _____ quickly.

d A lot of dot.coms don't really _____ anything.

e The present president didn't _____ the company, his father did.

f When did Nintendo _____ its subsidiary in the USA?

g Our objective is to _____ sales of $30 million this year.

h We want to _____ a new deal with our suppliers.

i The fastest way for the company to grow is to _____ smaller companies.

j Consultancies _____ services for other businesses.

k How much did your turnover _____ last year?

Answers on page 127

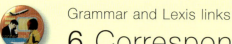

Grammar and Lexis links
6 Correspondence

Will for unplanned decisions

You use *will* + infinitive to show you are making an on-the-spot or new decision.

Practice 1 When would you say the following sentences? Match the decisions a–g to the situations 1–7.

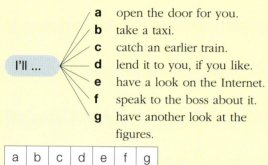

I'll ...
a open the door for you.
b take a taxi.
c catch an earlier train.
d lend it to you, if you like.
e have a look on the Internet.
f speak to the boss about it.
g have another look at the figures.

1 A customer asks if you can give him a better discount.
2 Your boss asks you if you can start work before the usual time.
3 A colleague reminds you about a meeting with a client on the other side of town in ten minutes.
4 Someone asks you where you can get a new battery for a laptop computer.
5 A colleague is carrying a lot of files and documents and has both hands occupied.
6 Your wife/husband asks if you can take a day off work.
7 A colleague admires a new CD you are listening to.

a	b	c	d	e	f	g

Practice 2 What would you say in these situations? Reply using the word in brackets.

a Someone offers you something to drink. You can have tea or coffee. (coffee)

b You are ordering a meal in a restaurant. You can have either soup or salad for a starter. (salad)

c You go out with some friends. You decide to pay for the drinks. (pay)

d A colleague who you like is having problems with a new computer program you are familiar with. (help)

e Someone reminds you that you are taking a flight at 10.30. It is now 9.15. (taxi).

f A colleague has heard on the radio that the buses are on strike and can't get home. You have your car. (lift).

Lexis: Business communication

Prepositions Match the parts of the sentences below.

a There is a message ...
b There is a mistake ...
c I asked him to phone ...
d I sent you an e-mail ...
e We confirmed the date of the meeting ...
f I will send you the packet ...
g I'd like to apologise ...
h We are giving top priority ...

1 ... in writing last week.
2 ... in the letter you sent me.
3 ... to your order form.
4 ... about this problem last week.
5 ... back this afternoon.
6 ... for what happened.
7 ... by courier this afternoon.
8 ... from Dave Cartwright for you.

a	b	c	d	e	f	g	h

Crossword Complete the crossword.
All the words are from unit 6.

Across

1. The _____ date for this order is June 26th. (when the order is supposed to arrive with the customer)
6. We'd like a _____ reply. ('quick' or 'fast')
8. People see e-mails as an _____ way of communicating. (the opposite of 'formal')
9. I'm sorry, I can't read his _____. (He wrote it with a pen.)
10. Machine used to send documents by telephone. (not a modem)
13. We hope to do more _____ with them in the future. (buy or sell things or services)
15. I need to look at the _____ again. (the noun of 'correspond')
19. To make sure something is correct.
21. Sometimes it's difficult to make a _____. (the noun of 'decide')
22. Could I leave a _____, please? (what you leave when someone is not there)
24. I'm really _____ he hasn't phoned me. (irritated)
28. 'Thank you.' 'You're _____.'
29. Could I take _____ the details? (the opposite of 'up')
30. Could you _____ that you have received this e-mail? (the verb of 'confirmation')

Down

2. Please do it _____. (at once)
3. The opposite of 'cheap'.
4. The name written at the bottom of a document.
5. Could you confirm the _____ in writing, please? (bits of information)
7. A service which picks up and delivers documents. (like UPS)
11. I'd like to _____ for the mistake. (say sorry)
12. I'm still waiting for a _____ from John to my letter.
14. Nowadays I use it for all my research and for sending e-mails.
16. I'm very _____ about this. (the adjective of 'worry')
17. I'm _____ about the order. (calling)
18. Error.
20. 'Hello, is _____ John?' 'Yes, speaking.'
23. Bad writing _____ cost companies a lot of money. (abilities)
25. I want to place an _____ for 300 units.
26. Can you _____ it to me by e-mail?
27. How much will it _____ us to send it?

Answers on page 128

Writing e-mails The following e-mails have arrived but there is a problem. There is no punctuation or capital letters. Correct the e-mails so that they make sense.

a dear mr gonzalez thank you for contacting lexington technical support unfortunately I do not understand the nature of the problem you are having or in fact even the product you are using can you please write back with as much information as you can about what product you are using what you are trying to do what problem you are having etc best regards kamal bouaissi technical support engineer

b dear richard tennant thank you for registering your lexington product your new customer number is 55563500 when calling technical support (925-253-3050) or lexington customer service (800-225-4880) please have your customer number ready we recommend writing your customer number in your lexington manual keeping it with our phone numbers and filing this e-mail for future reference thank you for your interest in lexington if there is anything we can do for you please let us know we will be happy to help you regards lexington customer service

Grammar and Lexis links
7 Making comparisons

Comparatives & superlatives

Adjective type	Adjective	Comparative	Superlative
1 syllable	rich cheap	rich**er** cheap**er**	the rich**est** the cheap**est**
1 syllable with 1 vowel + consonant	hot big	hot**ter** big**ger**	the hot**test** the big**gest**
2 syllables ending in -y	early heavy	ear**lier** heav**ier**	the ear**liest** the heav**iest**
2 syllables or more	economical interesting	**more** economical **more** interesting	**the most** economical **the most** interesting

You can often use the comparative form of adjectives with *than* to compare people, places and things.
- Life is **easier than** in the past.
- The company is **more profitable than** its competitors.

You can use *much, a lot, a bit* and *a little* to show if the differences are big or small.
- Mexico City is **a lot** bigger than Rome
- London is **much** more expensive than Madrid.

You can also use *not as ... as* to show differences.
- Travelling by train is **not as expensive as** by plane.

You use the article *the* with the superlative form of the adjective.
- Taking important decisions is **the hardest** part of management.
- **The most useful** aspect of the Internet is communication.

You can use *second, third* etc. with superlatives.
- Locally we are the **second** largest provider of Internet services.

You can also use *less ... than* and *the least* to show differences.
- Life in the past was **less** comfortable **than** it is now.
- His company is **the least** profitable on the stock exchange.

Practice 1 Rewrite the sentences using the opposite of the adjective.

a The Internet is faster than the post.
   The post is slower than the Internet.

b Hotels are more expensive than motels.
   Motels _____

c English is easier to learn than Chinese.
   Chinese _____

d Trains are more comfortable than buses.
   Buses _____

e People think that marketing is more interesting than accounting.
   People think that accounting _____

f Flying is safer than driving.
   Driving _____

g Small meetings are more efficient than large ones.
   Large meetings _____

h This job is better paid than my last one.
   My last job _____

i The economic situation is worse than it was four years ago.
   Four years ago the economic situation _____

Practice 2 *As* or *than*? Complete the sentences.

a The job isn't as interesting _____ I hoped.
b The journey was more expensive _____ I expected.
c This office has more space _____ the old one.
d I'm feeling more tired _____ yesterday.
e Fords aren't as good _____ Audis.

Practice 3 Complete the second sentence so that it means the same as the first sentence.

a It's easier to build hotels in the US than in Europe.
   It's not as difficult to build hotels in the US as it is in Europe.

b The Maserati GT is more powerful than the Chevrolet.
   The Chevrolet isn't _____
c The Chevrolet isn't as expensive as the Maserati.
   The Maserati is _____
d Profitability is more important than turnover.
   Turnover isn't _____
e Sales aren't as good as last year.
   Sales are _____
f This computer is faster than the old one.
   The old computer wasn't as _____
g It isn't as hot as yesterday.
   Yesterday _____

Practice 4 Who are the richest people in the world today? Look at the table below and complete the sentences. Has the situation changed since the information was published?

The 10 richest people in the world

1	Robson Walton	Country USA Business Retailing (Wal-Mart) Wealth in 2002 £73bn Wealth in 2001 £45.3bn
2	Bill Gates	Country USA Business Software (Microsoft) Wealth in 2002 £37.5bn Wealth in 2001 £37.5bn
3	Warren Buffett	Country USA Business Investments Wealth in 2002 £24.8bn Wealth in 2001 £17.3bn
4	Forrest Mars Jr	Country USA Business Confectionery Wealth in 2002 £19.2bn Wealth in 2001 £14bn
5	Karl & Theo Albrecht	Country Germany Business Supermarkets Wealth in 2002 £19bn Wealth in 2001 £13.3bn
6 =	Paul Allen	Country USA Business Software (Microsoft) Wealth in 2002 £17.8bn Wealth in 2001 £17bn
6 =	King Fahd	Country Saudi Arabia Business Oil Wealth in 2002 £17.8bn Wealth in 2001 £17.3bn
8	Larry Ellison	Country USA Business Computers (Oracle) Wealth in 2002 £16.7bn Wealth in 2001 £29bn
9	Barbara Cox Anthony & Anne Cox Chambers	Country USA Business Media Wealth in 2002 £14.3bn Wealth in 2001 £13.3bn
10	Prince Alwaleed	Country Saudi Arabia Business Investments Wealth in 2002 £14.2bn Wealth in 2001 £13.3bn

Adapted from The 50 Richest in the World, Forbes Magazine

In 2002 ...
a Robson Walton was the _____ person in the world.
b King Fahd wasn't _____ as Warren Buffett.
c Robson Walton was _____ Bill Gates.
d Warren Buffett was one of the _____ people in the world.
e Bill Gates was _____ before.
f Larry Ellison was _____ as in 2001.
g Paul Allen was _____ King Fahd.
h Most of the people in this list were _____ in 2001.

Lexis: Hotel services

1 Number the lines of the dialogue in the correct order.
   Receptionist
   ☐ Yes, sir. What would you like?
   ☐ Room service. Katherine speaking. Can I help you?
   ☐ Well, I'll have to ask in the kitchen to see if they have any *foie gras*. Would you like it with some toast?
   ☐ You're welcome, sir. Goodbye.
   ☐ Yes. Dry, medium or sweet?
   ☐ Right, sir. It will be with you in a few minutes.
   Guest
   ☐ Hello, Katherine. This is room 208 here. I'm feeling a bit hungry. I'd like to order a snack.
   ☐ Thank you, Katherine.
   ☐ Oh, as dry as possible, please, and nicely chilled.
   ☐ Oh, I don't know. Perhaps a little *foie gras*?
   ☐ Yes, please. And I'd also like some champagne.

2 Complete the sentences using the correct form of the words in brackets.
   a Some international hotel chains have a _____ database with information about their guests' preferences. (world)
   b If you call room service, they will _____ meals to your room. (delivery)
   c We can't afford to _____ any more staff. (employer)
   d A lot of our revenue comes from food and drink but our rooms are more _____. (profit)
   e Hotel guests from the USA _____ a standard room layout. (preference)
   f You can _____ old buildings into hotels but there is a limit to what you can do. (conversion)
   g We have to meet our customers' _____. (expect)
   h Multinational companies often expand by taking over smaller _____. (operate)

Grammar and Lexis links
9 Spirit of enterprise

Present Perfect

Affirmative		
I You We They	've (have)	finished the report.
He She	's (has)	

Negative		
I You We They	haven't	finished the report.
He She	hasn't	

Interrogative		
Have Has	I you we they	finished the report?
Has Hasn't	he she	

Short answers
Have you *seen* John?
Yes, I **have**. / No, I **haven't**.
Has Jane *sent* the letter?
Yes, she **has**. / No, she **hasn't**.

The past participle of regular verbs is the same as the Past Simple, but with many common irregular verbs it is different:
- go – went – **gone**
- come – came – **come**
- eat – ate – **eaten**

The tense you use to talk about past events depends on how you see them.
If you see actions and situations as part of a sequence of finished past events and situations (e.g. stages in your life, events in history, events in a narrative, etc.) you use the **Past Simple**.
- I **studied** economics at university.
- His first wife **was** Argentinean.
- Her last job **was** with an engineering firm.
- Bill Gates **founded** Microsoft with a friend.
- Some people **made** a lot of money in the war.
- Suddenly he **stopped** talking and left the room.

If past actions or situations are not related to other past events or time periods (they simply happened before now), you use the **Present Perfect**. Often it is because you are referring to recent events, or to contrast a present situation with the past.
- I've **had** a fantastic idea!
- We've **developed** a new product for our range.
- Our turnover **has grown** by 10%.
- The photocopier **has broken down**.

There is one important exception:
- *What did you say?* not ~~What have you said?~~

Practice 1 Write the past participles of the verbs below.

see _____   write _____
buy _____   break _____
sell _____   set _____
do _____   read _____
find _____   fall _____
come _____ rise _____
put _____   meet _____
take _____   think _____

Practice 2 Reorganise the words to make sentences in the Present Perfect.

a   lost   glasses   I   have   my
_____

b   gone   by   3%   prices   have   up
_____

c   has   stable   economic   remained   growth
_____

d   prices   last   years   have   in   fallen   five   the
_____

e   has   2,000   workers   sacked   Molinex
_____

f   company   has   the   Mr Rodriguez   left
_____

g   not   a   John   week   I   have   for   seen
_____

Practice 3 Write a sentence using the verbs in the box and the Present Perfect for the situations below.

| give   ~~stop~~   move   be   lose   arrive |
| change   break |

a   Half an hour ago it was raining and now it isn't.
    It's stopped raining.

b   The photocopier doesn't work. Half an hour ago it did.
    _____ down.

c   Ten minutes ago you called for a taxi. It's now outside the office.
    The taxi _____

d Last year your company was based on a site outside town. Now its offices are located in the centre of town.

_____ into the centre of town.

e You can't find your notes for a presentation.

_____ notes.

f You're giving a presentation. You did the same presentation last week and the week before.

This is the third time _____
_____

g Philip Windish works for a company. A week ago he worked for a different company.

_____

h A friend comments that nowadays he never sees you.

_____ very busy lately.

Practice 4 Match the questions to the answers.

a Where is my pen?
b Why are you looking so pleased with yourself?
c How is the new product line doing?
d Why are you looking for a new car?
e What's our share price today?
f Why are you looking so tired?
g Where's Jeremy?

1 It's gone up by four cents.
2 I've achieved my sales target for this month.
3 Because I've sold my old one.
4 It's been a really long day.
5 It's been very successful so far.
6 He's gone to Sydney for the week.
7 I don't know. I haven't seen it.

a	b	c	d	e	f	g

Practice 5 Complete the text with the verbs in the box, using either the Past Simple or the Present Perfect.

| reach | create | acquire | commence | add |
| increase | go | install | turn | launch |

The Inditex group consists of almost a hundred companies dealing with textile design, production and distribution. Its unique management techniques and its successes (a) _____ Inditex into one of the world's largest fashion groups.

Over the years the group (b) _____ other chains to the original Zara, each covering a different market sector. In 1991 the group (c) _____ Pull & Bear, and in 1995 (d) _____ 100% of Massimo Dutti. Bershka (e) _____ its activity in 1998, followed by the acquisition of Stradivarius in 1999. More recently, Inditex (f) _____ Oysho, a chain specialised in fashionable lingerie and underwear.

In the last four years the number of shops in the group (g) _____ a figure of over a thousand, and the group now has operations in 39 countries worldwide. In the same period, sales (h) _____ by 27% and net profits by 31%. In May 2001 the group was floated on the Madrid stock exchange and its share price (i) _____ from strength to strength.

Despite its size, the group still controls its activities from Arteixo, a village in the north west of Spain, where this year it (j) _____ its headquarters in a new building.

Answers on page 129

Lexis: Word building

Complete the table below with the appropriate form.

verb	noun	adjective
acquire	acquisition	acquired
reject	_____	rejected
grow	_____	growing
_____	success	_____
_____	_____	beneficial
innovate	_____	_____
_____	_____	flexible
_____	operation	operating
_____	_____	profitable
_____	increase	_____
_____	fall	fallen/falling
install	_____	installed

Grammar and Lexis links
10 Stressed to the limit

Have to

I / You / We / They	have to / don't have to	work at night.
He / She	has to / doesn't have to	
Do / Does	I/you/we/they he/she	have to work at night?

Should

I / You / He/She / We / They	should / shouldn't	do the job for free.

You use *has to/have to* to show that it is necessary to do something.
- Everyone **has to** pay taxes.
- We all **have to** use the same computer programs.

When you want to show that it isn't necessary to do something, you can use *doesn't have to/don't have to*.
- He **doesn't have to** travel much in his job.
- We **don't have to** dress formally for work.

You use *should* or *shouldn't* to show that it is a good or bad idea to do something.
- You **should** use the Internet for getting new ideas.
- You **shouldn't** work so hard if you want to live to an old age.

Practice 1 Complete the sentences in an appropriate way. Use *has to*, *have to*, *doesn't have to* or *don't have to* and the verbs in the box.

| get up | make | come | show | wear |
| finish | work | sign | get | do | go |

a All visitors to the factory _____ a register.
b Our company has a 'casual Friday' policy which means you _____ formal clothes in the office on Fridays.
c 'Why are you working so late?' 'Because I _____ this report for tomorrow.'
d To get to work on time he _____ at 5.30 a.m.

e Every Monday morning we _____ to a departmental meeting.
f I like holidays because you _____ anything.
g If you want to see Mr Smith you _____ an appointment. He's a very busy man.
h You _____ if you don't want to. We can do it without you.
i You _____ a visa if you travel to certain countries.
j When you cross an international border you usually _____ your passport.
k He's so rich he _____, but he still does. He's a workaholic.

Practice 2 Reorganise the words to make questions.
a finish   this   do   have   I   today   to
_____
b dress   do   have   work   for   to   you   formally
_____
c year   abroad   how   to   go   many   you   times   a   do   have
_____
_____
d complete   when   have   order   we   the   to   do
_____
e do   English   go   this   have   year   classes   we   to   to
_____
f your   have   drive   do   in   you   job   to   much
_____

Practice 3 Give appropriate advice using *should* or *shouldn't* and the verbs in the box.

| set up | leave | go | work | have | spend |
| ~~go~~ | | | | | |

a I can't get a job because I don't speak any foreign languages.
   <u>You should go to English classes.</u>
b I don't know how to use this new accountancy program.
   _____ on a course.

108   10 Grammar and Lexis link

c I keep getting these headaches.
_____ so much time staring at figures.

d My plane is at 2.30.
_____ or you'll miss it.

e I have this constant pain in my chest.
_____ a check-up.

f My family is complaining they never see me.
_____ so late.

g I don't like working for someone else.
_____ your own business.

Practice 4 Complete the sentences using a form of *have to* or *should* (affirmative or negative). Sometimes there are two possible answers.

a The doctor says I _____ take things easy.

b You _____ spend so much time in front of a computer – it's bad for your eyes.

c Managers _____ be good communicators.

d You _____ just give people orders, you _____ motivate them to do a good job.

e I _____ do this job even if it is stressful – I need the money.

f I'm going home now because I _____ get up early tomorrow to catch my plane.

g If you need travel information, you _____ look it up in the Internet.

h You _____ speak to the boss like that.

i If you want to know more about the company, you _____ visit them.

j You _____ come with me. I can do the presentation on my own.

Lexis: Stress at work

1 Complete the sentences with the correct form of the word in brackets.

a An air traffic controller has a very _____ job. (stress)

b A _____ has to answer the phone all day. (telephone)

c His work involves a lot of different _____. (responsible)

d Our boss is always shouting at us. I don't find it very _____. (motivate)

e Too much stress is bad for the workers, and it's also bad for the _____. (employ)

f Stress-related _____ is the cause of half of lost working days. (ill)

g It's a problem of _____ – we never know what's happening in the company. (communicate)

h Nobody knows how to use the new machine – we need urgent _____. (train)

i Employees shouldn't work under _____ pressure. (necessary)

j You should _____ your mistakes and correct them. (recognition)

k One of the benefits of reducing stress is better _____ with clients and colleagues. (relate)

l Workers need to rest and recuperate their _____ energies. (create)

m The experts say that bad _____ is the main cause of stress. (manage)

n Policies such as _____-related pay demotivate a work force. (perform)

2 Complete the second sentence so that it means the same as the first.

a Does your work cause you stress?
Do you find your work <u>stressful</u>?

b My boss makes life difficult.
My boss doesn't make life _____.

c My husband isn't very helpful.
My husband doesn't _____.

d At times I get nervous.
At times I get a bit on _____.

e 75% of visits to the doctor are because of stress.
75% of visits to the doctor are the _____ of stress.

f People don't think that teaching is a difficult job. Everyone thinks that teaching is an _____.

g I hope things improve for you.
I hope things get _____ for you.

h Worrying about things doesn't help you.
There's _____ in worrying about things.

i I don't work for anyone. I'm self-employed.
I work for _____.

Grammar and Lexis links
11 Top jobs

Present Perfect – the unfinished past

You use the Present Perfect to say when present situations began. For example:
Past Simple: *I started working here 25 years ago.*
Present Simple: *I work here now.*
Present Perfect: *I've **worked** here for 25 years.*
NOT ~~I am working here for 25 years.~~ *

Past Simple: *I met John for the first time in 1985.*
Present Simple: *I still know him.*
Present Perfect: *I've **known** John since 1985.*
NOT ~~I know John since 1985.~~ *

* In many languages, you use a present tense to express this idea so these are very common mistakes. In English you can only use the Present Perfect.

To say when the action began you use *since* or *for*. You use *since* with a point in time and *for* with a period of time.

since	for
8 o'clock	2 years
1975	a month
August	a few minutes
last week	half an hour
I was born	ages
he arrived	hundreds of years

*Things have been better **since** we changed offices.*
*He has lived here **for** ten years.*
NOT ... ~~since ten years ago.~~

You can also use *for* with the Past Simple. Compare these sentences:
Present Perfect: *I've **lived** in Manchester **for** three years / **since** 1998.* (I still live in Manchester.)
Past Simple: *I **lived** in Manchester **for** three years / **from** 1995 **to** 1998.* (Now I live somewhere else.)

Practice 1 Complete the sentences with *since* or *for*.

a   Mr Bianchi has been out of the office _____ last Thursday.
b   We haven't had a holiday _____ the summer.
c   They have been friends _____ they were at university together.
d   He's had his own business _____ a few years now.
e   I haven't seen you _____ a while. How are things going?
f   I've known Pete _____ we met at a trade fair nearly ten years ago.
g   They've had that old car _____ years.
h   Mr Gonzalez has been here _____ 9.30. He's waiting for you in reception.
i   _____ his wife had a baby, he's spent more time at home.
j   He's waited for this promotion _____ months.

Practice 2 Write questions with *How long ...?* and the Present Perfect.

a   you / work / here
    How long have you worked here?
b   he / know / about this problem
    _____
c   she / be / a director of the company
    _____
d   you / want / change jobs
    _____
e   they / have / their website
    _____
f   he / be / interested / in working for us
    _____
g   he / have / a company car
    _____
h   she / be / responsible for that account
    _____

Practice 3 Rewrite the following sentences using the Present Perfect.

a   He works here – he started work in January.
    He's worked here since January.
b   He lives in Paris – he was born there.
    _____
c   He's a computer programmer – he became a programmer when he left university.
    _____
d   They make furniture – they started making furniture over a hundred years ago.
    _____
e   She owns a business – she set it up five years ago.
    _____
f   They lead the market – they became market leaders in 1998. _____

Practice 4 Rewrite the following sentences using the Present Perfect.

a I met him at university.
   I've known him since university.

b Mr Jones arrived here hours ago.

c When did you buy your car?

d I got this job in January.

e They told me about the problem yesterday.

f They got divorced two years ago.

Practice 5 Read the biographical details of James Brown. Then use the prompts to write sentences using either the Present Perfect or the Past Simple and *for*, *since*, or *from ... to*.

James Brown

1974	started smoking
1976	went to university to study engineering
1979	graduated with a degree in engineering
1980	got a job with Rolls Royce as an aeronautical engineer
1981	became interested in boats
1982	got married
1983	bought his first yacht
1985	got a job with P & W in Canada and moved to Montreal
1991	moved back to the UK and went to work at the P & W factory in Manchester
1993	gave up smoking
1996	moved to a new job in the P & W offices in Portsmouth

a be / an aeronautical engineer
   He's been an aeronautical engineer since 1980.

b smoke

c study engineering / university

d be / interested / boats

e be / married

f work / Rolls Royce

g have / yacht

h live / Canada

i live / the UK

j have / job / Portsmouth

k work / for P & W

l not smoke

Lexis: Company news

Match the parts of the sentences.

a Dan Colman graduated from York University in 1980 with ...
b He and some student friends founded ...
c In 1998 they moved ...
d At the beginning it was a small firm which produced components ...
e The company quickly expanded and set ...
f Recently, it has launched ...
g The engineers responsible ...
h It has also entered the ...
i Dan Colman has held ...
j The company has recently celebrated ...

1 ... for other manufacturers.
2 ... mobile phone market.
3 ... the top position since it was founded.
4 ... a degree in electronic engineering.
5 ... a range of computer accessories, which is doing very well.
6 ... it's twentieth anniversary.
7 ... up new divisions.
8 ... its headquarters to Milton Keynes.
9 ... for this success have become directors of the company.
10 ... the company ALTS in 1982.

a	b	c	d	e	f	g	h	i	j

Grammar and Lexis links
13 Air travel

Conditionals with *will*

If + Present, *will/won't* + infinitive
- If I **have** time, I'**ll finish** the figures this afternoon.
- If they **don't offer** me more money, I **won't accept** the job.

Will/won't + infinitive + *if* + Present
- He **won't wait** if you **arrive** late.
- I'**ll phone** you if I my mobile **works** there.

You can use conditionals with *will* to talk about future events which depend on other things happening.

Practice 1 Match the parts of the sentences.
a If you don't leave now, ...
b You'll be late ...
c If I get a promotion, ...
d I'll buy a better car ...
e If people are rude to BA ground staff, ...
f If we make a good offer, ...
g I'll take longer to get to the airport ...
h I'll put on weight ...
i If you don't have any plans for tonight, ...
j They'll get more work done ...

1 ... they won't be able to get on the plane.
2 ... if I go to so many business lunches.
3 ... you'll miss your flight.
4 ... if you don't keep interrupting them.
5 ... if you don't call a taxi now.
6 ... if we coincide with the rush hour.
7 ... I'll earn more money.
8 ... if they increase my salary.
9 ... will you have dinner with me?
10 ... we'll get the contract.

a	b	c	d	e	f	g	h	i	j

Practice 2 Complete the sentences using one of the verbs below in the correct tense.

| phone | find | lose | pay | improve | be |
| need | adopt | have | tell | | |

a If I see John, I _____ him what you said.
b If anyone _____ to contact me, tell them I'll be back at four.
c We _____ able to get the 10.14 train if we hurry.
d If you _____ my keys, will you let me know?
e Your English _____ if you spend some time in the USA.
f I _____ you if there's any news.
g If we _____ within 30 days, will you drop the price?
h If BA's policy on rude passengers is a success, other airlines _____ it.
i If he checks in late, he _____ his seat assignment.
j You _____ to hurry if you want to catch you flight.

Practice 3 Write a sentence using the conditional with *will* based on each piece of advice.

a You should confirm your booking or you won't get a good seat.
   If you confirm your booking, you'll get a good seat.
b You should pretend you're not interested in buying from them or they won't drop the price.
   _____
   _____
c You should apologise to the boss or you will have problems.
   _____
   _____
d You shouldn't drink too much on the flight or you'll have to keep going to the toilet.
   _____
   _____
e You should leave for the airport now or you'll miss your flight.
   _____
   _____
f You shouldn't 'get stroppy' with the ground staff or they won't let you on the plane.
   _____
   _____
g You should study something practical or you won't get a job.
   _____
   _____

h You shouldn't work so hard as you do or you'll get ill.

_____

_____

i You should take the client out to lunch or you won't get his business.

_____

_____

Lexis: Negotiating & air travel

Negotiation Complete the dialogue with the words in the box.

10%	price	accept	do	business
up	deal	deliver	discount	payment
order	more			

A Okay, we want to do (a) _____ with you, but we need to talk about the (b) _____.

B Well, the catalogue price is $30.25.

A I know, but we're talking about a big (c) _____ here. If we order 100 units, for example, what (d) _____ will you give me?

B If you order (e) _____ than 100 units, I'll give you a discount of (f) _____.

A 10%. And for 150 units?

B For 150 units, I'll go (g) _____ to 12%.

A 12%. That sounds good. What about (h) _____?

B Payment is within 60 days.

A Er, if you let us pay within 90 days, I'll (i) _____ a lower discount ... say 10% on 150 units.

B So, you're saying that if I offer a discount of 10% on the catalogue price for an order of 150 units, with payment within 90 days, we'll have a (j) _____?

A Yes, we'll have a deal ... if you can (k) _____ in two weeks.

B All right, then. I think we can (l) _____ that. It's a deal!

Air travel

1 Imagine you are flying from Europe to the USA. Number the following events in a logical order.

- [1] **a** Book your flight over the Internet or by phoning the airline.
- [ ] **b** Check in at least 45 minutes before your flight.
- [ ] **c** Go through the metal detector and wait for your flight to be announced.
- [ ] **d** Fasten your seat belt and take off.
- [ ] **e** Show your boarding pass at the boarding gate and get on the plane.
- [ ] **f** Check the details of your reservation and seat assignment.
- [ ] **g** Dominate the armrests!
- [ ] **h** Go through customs.
- [ ] **i** Take a taxi to your hotel.
- [ ] **j** Land at JFK airport and get off the plane.
- [ ] **k** Go through passport control and pick up luggage in baggage reclaim.

2 Match the parts of the sentences.

a You should ask for the seat you want when you book ...
b It's important to tackle ...
c There was a traffic jam and I missed ...
d The flight was overbooked so they offered me ...
e If he gets stroppy, don't pay ...
f I don't think the new BA rules will solve ...

1 ... your flight
2 ... my flight.
3 ... the problem of air rage.
4 ... any attention to him.
5 ... problems before they get too big.
6 ... a refund or a later flight.

a	b	c	d	e	f

Grammar and Lexis links
14 Hiring and firing

The passive

The object in active sentences becomes the subject in passive sentences.

Active
Someone **services** the machine every year.
They **have closed down** five factories.
They **decorated** the offices last year.
They'**ve closed** the old factory.
They **are encouraging** her to apply for the job.
They **don't clean** the office on Friday.

Passive (*to be* + past participle)
The machine **is serviced** every year.
Five factories **have been closed down**.
The offices **were decorated** last year.
The old factory **has been closed**.
She **is being encouraged** to apply for the job.
The office **isn't cleaned** on Friday.

You often use the passive to put the important information at the beginning of a sentence. The passive can be more impersonal than the active. For this reason, you can use it in formal documents such as reports.

You can use *by* to emphasise who or what performed an action.
- The book was written **by** Peter Hudson.
- The equipment is damaged **by** prolonged exposure to sunlight.

Practice 1 Reorganise the words to make correct sentences.

a June was at the contract the signed end of
_____

b sacked slowly Sheila was working too for
_____

c damaged fire the the in was office
_____

d workers accident injured were the in some
_____

e measures announced the have new been
_____

f staff employed new no year this be will
_____

g redesigned corporate is image being our
_____

h salaries increased year have this been our
_____

Practice 2 Rewrite the sentences in the passive.

a They have cancelled the order.
   <u>The order has been cancelled.</u>

b They haven't finished the new building.
   _____

c Someone told him about the meeting.
   _____

d Someone stole the plans for the new engine.
   _____

e Someone will pick you up at the airport.
   _____

f They didn't ask him if he wanted the job.
   _____

g Did anyone tell you about what happened at the meeting? _____

h They hold a sales conference every year.
   _____

i Something delayed his flight.
   _____

j They are answering the complaints in writing.
   _____

Practice 3 Answer the questions using a sentence in the passive and *by*.

a Who was the inventor of the light bulb?
   <u>The light bulb was invented by Thomas Edison.</u>

b What currency was the replacement for the peseta, franc and lira in 2002?
   _____

c How many countries form the United Kingdom?
   _____

d Who is the author of this book?
   _____

e Who is the owner of this book?
   _____

f What type of heating have you got in your office – oil, gas or electric?
   _____

g Who was the director of the film *Some Like it Hot?*
_____
_____

h Which company was the original manufacturer of the PC? _____
_____

Answers at foot of page

Lexis: Procedures

1 Match the parts of the sentences.

a She was employed ...
b The incident was reported ...
c John was consulted ...
d The staff have been informed ...
e She was sacked ...
f The conditions were agreed ...
g He didn't accept the offers which were put ...
h The worker was injured ...
i The flight was delayed ...
j The passive is used ...

1 ... on a temporary basis.
2 ... about the decision.
3 ... for writing reports.
4 ... for stealing office stationery.
5 ... to him by the employment office.
6 ... by the bad weather.
7 ... to the supervisor.
8 ... at a company wide level.
9 ... of the new working hours.
10 ... by an explosion in the chemical plant.

a	b	c	d	e	f	g	h	i	j

2 Combine one word from box A with one word from box B to complete each sentence below.

A	B
electronics	application
written	secrets
job	position
company	rights
workers'	needs
job	security
previous	workers
skilled	warning
temporary	staff
unemployment	benefits
staffing	industry

a For young people _____ is not usually as important as a good salary.
b We gave the employee a _____ for arriving late to work two days running.
c In the summer there is more work so we have to take on more people to meet our _____.
d He was accused of revealing _____ to a competitor.
e A hundred years ago _____ didn't exist because there were no unions.
f You always have to include a CV in your _____.
g Education is important because industry needs a supply of _____.
h Was your _____ a full-time post?
i In many countries there are no _____ for people who have no work.
j At Christmas, shops take on _____ because it's a busy time of year.
k The _____ is an important sector of the local economy.

3 Reorganise the letters to form words to complete the sentences.

| kasc | veritwine | kemart | girinf |
| dali fof | revbal | nowd | |

a Two hundred workers at the factory have been _____ because of the bad financial situation.
b This mobile phone is the smallest on the _____.
c I asked her to put the phone _____ and come into my office.
d They can't _____ you without giving you at least two warnings in writing.
e _____ someone is one of the most difficult things a manager has to do.
f The first thing you have to do is give the employee a _____ warning.
g How did your _____ go, then? Do you think you got the job?

Answers (Practice 3)
b euro c four d Simon Clarke
g Billy Wilder h IBM

Grammar and Lexis links
15 Time

Going to vs will

be + *going to* + infinitive

I	am / 'm not	
You / We / They	are / aren't	going to apply for the job.
He / She	is / isn't	

| Are(n't) | you / they / we | |
| Is(n't) | he / she | going to phone later? |

You can use *going to* to talk about intentions and decisions you have made about the future before the moment of speaking.
- We're *going to* open a new office in Berlin.
- I'm *going to* ask for an application form for the new post.

Going to or *will*?
You use *will* to show you are making a decision at the moment of speaking.
A Could I speak to Mr Gomez, please?
B I'm afraid he's out at the moment. Can I take a message?
A No thanks, **I'll phone** later.

Practice 1 Write sentences using *going to* and the word prompts.

a this evening / meet / friends / a drink.
   This evening I'm going to meet some friends for a drink.

b they / employ / more staff / deal with the new order
   _____
   _____

c you / meet / me / airport?
   _____

d what / you / say / at / meeting?
   _____

e next year / I / study / German
   _____

f he / look for / new job
   _____

g she / not / accept / our offer
   _____

h we / take / train / bus?
   _____

Practice 2 Complete the responses with the verb in brackets using either *going to* or *will*.

a We've run out of toner for the photocopier.
   Have we? I _____ (order) some more.

b What are your plans for the weekend?
   We _____ (visit) some friends in the country. Do you want to come?

c Did you remember to book the hotel?
   No, I forgot! I _____ (phone) now. I hope they still have some room.

d You should consult George about the production problems.
   I've already mentioned it to him. We _____ (discuss) it this afternoon.

e Have you seen their offices? They're miles from anywhere in this really old building.
   Yes, I know. But they _____ (move) to a new place next year.

f I'm dying for a cup of coffee.
   All right, I _____ (make) one now. Do you take sugar?

g Why are you working so hard?
   Because I _____ (leave) on time today, for a change, and I want to finish this before I go.

h I have to go to the airport and my car won't start.
   Don't worry. I _____ (lend) you mine.

Practice 3 Complete the conversation using the words in the box.

start	information	time	do	urgent
easier	strategy	someone	learn	

A   What are you doing?

B   I'm putting this customer (a) _____ into the database.

A   Why don't you get (b) _____ else in your team to do it?

B   Well, it's (c) _____ if I just do it myself.

A   Yes, but if you do it yourself, they'll never (d) _____.

B   Yes, you're probably right. I'll (e) _____ that next time.

A   Anyway, have you finished the marketing (f) _____ for the new product launch?

B   No, I'm going to (g) _____ that this afternoon.

A   Oh, come on! It's really (h) _____. We're all waiting for it.

B   I know, but I haven't had (i) _____.

Lexis: Working conditions

1 Combine one word from box A with one word from box B to complete each sentence below.

A	B
realistic	planning
eight-hour	deadline
long	forecasts
sales	line
forward	hours
bottom	day

a   Monday is too soon for us: next Friday is a more _____.

b   The traditional _____ does not suit our natural daily rhythm.

c   According to our _____ we are going to sell over 20% more next year.

d   In any business the _____ is that you have to make enough money to survive.

e   You should give priority to important tasks such as _____ and problem analysis.

f   In the UK, people work _____ but their productivity is not as high as in France or Germany.

2 Complete the sentences using the correct form of the words in brackets.

a   Most people _____ better in the morning. (performance)

b   A psychologist is going to _____ the staff to see how they work. (observation)

c   Time management _____ will not be impressed by the results of the experiment. (specialise)

d   We are not so _____ after a good lunch. (production)

e   They _____ to reduce the working week to 35 hours in some countries. (intention)

f   Have you _____ what to do about the situation? (decision)

g   The _____ went on for hours and the meeting ended very late. (discuss)

"You're always so busy, Carter. You come to work early, you leave late. What are you up to?"

Grammar and Lexis links
17 Office gossip

Reported speech

Say & tell

You can use *say* or *tell* to report what someone said.

say + something
- He **says** (that) he is happy in his new job.

tell + somebody + something
- He **tells** everyone (that) he is the company boss.

Tense

If you use the past forms *said* or *told*, you have to change the verbs in the original.

Present → past
- I **like** working on my own. → He said he **liked** working on his own.

Will → *would*:
- I**'ll** help you. → He said he **would** help me.

Pronouns

I → he/she
me → him/her
my → his/her
your → my
- **I** speak to **your** secretary every day. →
  He told me **he** spoke to **my** secretary every day.

Adverbs of time & place

now → then/at that moment
today → that day
here → there
tomorrow → the next day/the following day
yesterday → the day before/the previous day
- I'll see you **here tomorrow**. → He said he would see me **there the next day**.

Most of these changes are logical and natural and often similar in other languages. They depend on the differences in time, place and people between the original conversation and the reported conversation.

Asked

For reported questions you can use *asked* + *what/when/*etc.
- What do you want? →
  He **asked** me *what* I wanted.

or *asked* + *if* for reporting yes/no questions.
- Is it official? →
  He **asked** me *if* it was official.

Practice 1 Complete the second sentence to report the first one.

a I'm really enjoying my job at the moment.
   She says <u>she's really enjoying her job at the moment.</u>

b It's too late to cancel the meeting.
   I said _____

c We are having a lot of problems with the production department today.
   He told me _____
   _____

d What time is Mr Keegan going to arrive?
   He asked _____

e We should buy a new computer system.
   He keeps telling me _____
   _____

f Is Mr Marchain available?
   She asked _____

g The fixed costs include the office rent and equipment hire.
   She said _____
   _____

h Where do you work now?
   They asked me _____

i I'll meet you at the airport at eight o'clock.
   She said _____
   _____

j I want to see you about the arrangements for tomorrow.
   He told me _____
   _____

k Does the office open on Saturdays?
   He asked me _____

l When will the documents be ready?
   She asked _____

m I'm the best salesman in the company.
   He keeps saying _____
   _____

n Can I make a phone call?
   He asked if _____

o What do you think of the new website?
   He asked me _____
   _____

Practice 2 Complete the sentences with *say/said*, *tell/told*, or *ask/asked*.

a Why didn't you _____ me you weren't happy with your job?
b What will people _____ if we try to ban office gossip?
c Did he _____ what time you had to be there?
d The boss always _____ that I should keep my desk more organised.
e He _____ me he was having second thoughts about applying for the job.
f Will you _____ him if he's going to come?
g I can't read the small print on this. What does it _____?
h Every time I visit them they _____ me how you are.
i I'll _____ you if you promise not to _____ anything to anybody else.

Lexis: Relationships at work

1 Combine one word from box A with one word from box B to complete each sentence below.

A	B
coffee	consultant
company	room
human	policy
meeting	resources
management	machine

a People have the best ideas in conversations around the _____.
b The company has hired a _____ to give advice on improving internal communications.
c What do you think about this idea of removing the chairs from the _____ so we don't spend so long talking about things?
d What is the _____ on taking coffee or tea breaks?
e Nowadays people say _____ instead of 'personnel'.

2 Complete the puzzle using the clues below. Sometimes the first letter has been given.

1 Having communal areas benefits relations in the w___.
2 We are having a ___ for efficiency. (You also ___ a car.)
3 What this unit is about.
4 Let's make an ___ not to waste time.
5 It's not a good idea to ___ rumours.
6 Have you heard the ___?
7 There's no ___ without fire.
8 We have banned smoking in the o___.
9 They don't a___ of people taking long tea breaks.
10 Let's go to the pub for a ___ on Friday night.
11 We should encourage employees to ___ their ideas.
12 What has happened to the tea ___?

"The whole company is being relocated but nobody will tell me where to."

Grammar and Lexis links
18 E-commerce

Will for future predictions

Affirmative		
I you he she it we they	will ('ll)	work

Negative		
I you he she it we they	will not (won't)	work

Interrogative		
will won't	I you he she it we they	work?

The negative of *will* is *won't*.
- I'm sorry, but things **won't get** any better.
- No, there **won't be** a recession.

Put *will* before the subject to make questions.
- **Will** people **use** the Internet for most of their shopping in the future?
- **Will** the economy **recover** by next year?

You often introduce predictions with *I think* ...
- *I think* the DVD **will replace** the CD.
- *I think* the meeting **will end** on time.

Avoid saying *I think ... won't ...*
Use *I don't think ... will ...*
- *I don't think* the keyboard **will become** obsolete.
  (NOT ~~I think the keyboard won't become obsolete~~.)
- *I don't think* the meeting **will end** on time.
  (NOT ~~I think the meeting won't end on time~~.)

You can use *will* + infinitive to express predictions or beliefs about the future.
- *This year the economy **will grow** by 3%.*
- *I'm sure we **will finish** the order on time.*

Practice 1 Join the sentence beginnings with the endings using *will* + the verbs in the box.

have ~~continue~~ take get affect be go retire arrive

a Prices ... — will continue — ... public by next year.
b There ... ... with a massive golden handshake soon.
c The managing director ... ... better.
d The government ... ... a boom in the economy.
e Young George ... ... late as usual.
f The company ... ... measures against inflation.
g Life here ... ... a very successful career, I'm sure.
h The plane ... ... to rise.
i The political situation ... ... the economy.

Practice 2 Reorganise the words to make correct sentences.

a any new you system won't with have problems the
   You won't have any problems with the new system.

b information think the Internet I you'll on find the
   _____

c Berlin you'll good have time think I a in
   _____

d Juan Montes think see you'll there don't I
   _____

e think do write report time you'll the you to have?
   _____

f time you what arrive will?
   _____

g long how us it will get there take to?
   _____

h we'll shopping I to think go time any don't have
   _____

i make think money I he'll lot a of

_____

j want people see buy will always to products they before them most

_____
_____

Practice 3 Make questions with *do you think ... will ...?* and then write answers that are true for you.

a What time / get home tonight?

<u>What time do you think you'll get home tonight? About 7.30.</u>

b What / have / dinner?

_____
_____

c Where / go / next holiday?

_____
_____

d change / jobs / next five years?

_____
_____

e lose / weight / this month?

_____
_____

f How long / take / do this exercise?

_____
_____

g ever have / own business?

_____
_____

h ever drive / Ferrari?

_____
_____

i work as hard / five years from now?

_____
_____

Lexis: Shopping & the Internet

Collocations Match each verb on the left to the item on the right that it collocates with. Then use the phrases to complete the sentences.

compare	a bill
influence	the conversation
listen to	a network
run up	prices
try on	the decision
access	a sweater

a I like to _____ before I buy anything expensive.

b His children have _____ of over $300 by surfing on the Internet all day long.

c When she asked to _____, they told her they didn't have one in her size.

d To _____ you have to obtain a user name and a password from the administrator.

e Did you _____ in the canteen yesterday?

f What factors do you think will most _____ on salaries?

Buying online Complete the anecdote using the words in the box.

crashed	website	message	security	came
e-mail	complain	online	reply	button
charge	pay	download	clicked	

Why I will never buy anything on the Internet again

Ask most people how shopping will be in the future and inevitably they will mention the Internet. Well, the other day I had a bad enough experience shopping (a) _____ to put me off for life. I heard about a book you could download from a (b) _____ before it was published and sold in bookshops. As it was by an author I adore, I decided to investigate.

I found the page and read the information. They charged sixty euros for the (c) _____. Not a massive amount but you had to use a credit card. I completed the form with the endless details requested, including my (d) _____ address. Finally I entered my credit card number, because they solemnly promised that there was no (e) _____ risk. When the payment was authorised – it took about a minute – a new screen appeared with a (f) _____ which said 'download now'. I (g) _____ on the button but nothing happened so I clicked again. Then a (h) _____ came up saying 'Download suspended due to network overload. Please try again later.'

Finally the system (i) _____ and I had to turn off the computer. When I reconnected, the same forms as before (j) _____ up but I didn't want to risk paying again, so I wrote an e-mail to the company explaining the problem. I never got a (k) _____.

I assumed that as I never got the book I wouldn't have to (l) _____, but when I got my credit card statement at the end of the month I saw the (m) _____ for sixty euros was there. It was too late to do anything and there was no one to (n) _____ to. Okay, so it was only sixty euros – no big deal – but the question I ask myself is this: why risk buying online when it amounts to what is basically an act of faith? In any case, it will be a long time before I try buying something over the Internet again.

Grammar and Lexis links
19 Working from home

Conditionals (future reference)

You can use *if* + past + *would/could* to talk about hypothetical or imagined situations in the future. This is often called the 'second conditional'. Look at these examples:

Condition   **Consequence**
If I **knew** the answer,   **I'd tell** you.
If we **got** the order,   **we'd have** years of work.

Compare these two sentences:
- **If** the factory **shuts**, over 200 people **will lose** their jobs.
  (The speaker thinks the situation is likely to happen in the future.)
- **If** the factory **shut**, over 200 people **would lose** their jobs.
  (The speaker thinks the situation is unlikely or improbable in the future.)

Practice 1 Match the parts of the following conditional sentences.

a If we worked from home, ...
b If I spent less time travelling, ...
c The company would save money ...
d People would need good computers ...
e Our quality of life would improve ...
f If I never saw my colleagues, ...
g There'd be problems with this plan ...

1 ... I'd have more time with my family.
2 ... if the staff didn't agree with it.
3 ... if they had to work from home.
4 ... if we didn't have to commute.
5 ... I'd miss the personal contact.
6 ... we'd spend less time travelling.
7 ... if it invested in home working.

a	b	c	d	e	f	g

Practice 2 David and Sarah are a couple who live in London with their two young children. Read their conversation and complete it using the verb in brackets in the appropriate tense.

Sarah Why don't we move out of the city into the country? I'm fed up with living here. It's so stressful.
David If we (a) _____ (live) in the country, it (b) _____ (take) about ten minutes for you to get bored with it.
Sarah No it wouldn't. We (c) _____ (get) a nice big house – somewhere with a garden. The kids (d) _____ (go) to a little village school, and we (e) _____ (forget) about all the street violence, traffic and pollution.
David But they (f) _____ (like) living in the city, and they (g) _____ (miss) their friends. Also, if we (h) _____ (move) into the country, we (i) _____ (spend) all our time in the car travelling in and out to work.
Sarah Not necessarily. If you (j) _____ (ask) your company, they (k) _____ (let) you work from home some of the time, and mine would to.
David I don't think so. I (l) _____ (have) to be in contact with people in my job. Anyway, if I (m) _____ (be) in the house all day, I (n) _____ (go) crazy.
Sarah Don't be so negative. If you (o) _____ (spend) more time at home, we (p) _____ (see) more of you, and we could do more things like going for walks and playing tennis. You (q) _____ (have) a better quality of life.
David I'm sorry. I just don't think you're being realistic. It (r) _____ (be) a dream.
Sarah If you (s) _____ (be) less selfish, you'd at least think about it.
David Okay, I promise I (t) _____ (give) it some thought if that's what you want.

Practice 3 Write conditional sentences using the prompts.

a He doesn't work hard so he isn't very successful.
   <u>If he worked harder, he'd be more successful.</u>
b You don't have enough experience so we can't give you the job. _____
   _____
c He can't drive so he has to take taxis all the time.
   _____
   _____
d I don't have the information so I can't help you.
   _____
   _____

e I don't like sport so I don't go to the gym.
_____

f He works long hours because he enjoys his job.
_____
_____

g She only does the job because she hasn't got any choice. _____
_____

h My car is in the garage so I can't take you to the airport. _____
_____

i Things take him a long time because he isn't very organised. _____

j He drives an expensive car because he can afford it.
_____
_____

Practice 4 Give advice by completing the sentences.

a If you got up earlier, <u>you wouldn't be late to work so often.</u>

b If you did a computer course, _____
_____

c You would make a better impression _____
_____

d If you had a mobile phone, _____
_____

e You wouldn't be so stressed _____
_____

f If you used the Internet, _____
_____

g You'd do better at the interview _____
_____

h If you didn't complain all the time, _____
_____

Practice 5 Reorganise the words to form questions.

a job do what would you if choose you could

<u>What job would you do if you could choose?</u>

b live you abroad you where if would to had go

c treat people boss how you would were if you the

d didn't language study would what you English you if learn
_____
_____

e would earn how a you the wasn't living salary if important
_____
_____

Lexis: Teleworking

The text below is an extract from an article about teleworking. Complete it using the words in the box.

desk   home   flexibility   office   local   commute

'The key word for the future is (a) _____. We're not suddenly going to see massive numbers of people working from (b) _____ instead of going into the (c) _____. We'll see a much more hybrid existence where some of the time people are in the office, maybe at a shared (d) _____, and some of the time at home. And there are of course 'telecentres' – serviced offices which provide an intermediate stage where people can find a (e) _____ office instead of having to (f) _____ into a town or city centre.'

Additional material

1 Selling your company
Jon Day's verdict on Moonpig (p6, ex7)

There are two types of Internet business models that I like – ones that solve an existing problem, such as Tesco.com, which delivers bulky grocery items to my door, and those that could not exist without the Internet, such as the eBay auction site. Moonpig has elements of both. It offers a convenient way to select greetings cards without going to a shop and allows the cards to be customised, a possibility the Internet opens up.

While investigating Moonpig I ordered a few cards and found the service to be user-friendly and the personalisation of cards a unique selling point. My biggest concern is their estimated cost of converting offline customers to online customers. To reach their target of 750,000 customers would cost almost £10 million.

My score: 7.5/10

Answers: Lexis link (p95, crossword)

Across
2   website
3   list
5   e-mail
7   mouse
9   intranet
10 link
11 connection
14 virus
16 browse

Down
1   attachment
4   screen
6   download
8   online
12 click
13 site
15 surf

2 Women in business
Statistics (p10, ex2)

Women in the workplace

- 46.5% of US labour force
- 49.5% of middle management positions
- 12.5% of senior managers
- 11.7% of board directors
- 4.1% of top earners
- 2 Fortune 500 CEOs

3 Telephone talk
Customer frustration (p17, ex2)

The five main frustrations customers experience in dealing with telephone staff are:
- taking too long to answer
- being put on hold and forgotten
- being transferred and having to repeat their enquiry
- being answered by voicemail and other machines
- not having calls returned

Indirect questions (p18, ex2)

A   InterAir / help?
B   Yes, please / like / information / flight / Munich
A   Yes / know / flight number?
B   The flight number? / sure / know / leaves Munich / 1730
A   yes / IA 345
B   Yes / tell / time / gets in?
A   arrival / 1910
B   1910 / know / delay?
A   No / flight / on time
B   Right / thank / much
A   welcome / goodbye

4 Networking
Answers (p21, ex4)

a   Who do you work for?
b   Where is your company based?
c   Where are you staying?
d   Do you speak (*German*)?
e   Who is (*Alex*) talking to?
f   What do you do? / What's your job?
g   Have you got any children? / Do you have any children?
h   Where are you from? / Where do you come from?
i   Are you married?
j   Do you play golf?
k   Do you know (*Adriana Bellini*)?

15 Time

Wasting time (p72, ex4)

Be sloppy

A good hour or two can be gained every few weeks if you keep your desk in a mess. Friday afternoons and Monday mornings are perfect times to set aside for cleaning up your work area. (28 minutes to an hour once a week)

The computer

Load your computer with unnecessary programs that make your machine run more slowly. While you're waiting for the PC to process information, sit back and relax. If the boss questions you, just say, 'Damn computers.' He'll laugh and agree with you. (roughly 42 minutes a day)

The Internet

Be very careful misusing the company PC to surf the Net for personal enjoyment. Your boss knows the Internet is a big waste of time and is watching for people who are doing web searches for MP3s and games. The best way is to use it for all research. If you need a phone number for a client across town, use the Internet to find it. Most people just reach for a phone book, which is faster than using the Internet. (roughly 9 to 33 minutes a day.)

Office conversations

Enter business conversations around the office that are taking place in the open. You don't have to be a part of the conversation very much. The important thing is to be there physically. Just listen and nod your head when appropriate. (23 minutes to 1.3 hours)

Meetings

Go to every meeting you can get into. You'd be surprised at how many people miss the opportunity to waste time by avoiding meetings. Once you're in a meeting, it's all about planning your weekend, or thinking about the football game you watched the night before. (According to Office Studies International the average meeting takes 42 minutes and meetings happen every 5 hours. Count on 2–3 meetings a week).

Adapted from 'Wasting time at work' by Galen Black

18 E-commerce

Sentences for comparison (p81, ex1)

a   When you buy something for yourself with your own money, you're interested in quality and price.

b   When you buy something for someone else with your own money, you're interested in price.

c   When you buy something for yourself with someone else's money, you're interested in quality.

d   When you buy something for someone else with someone else's money, who cares?

19 Working from home

Teleworking (p89, ex5)

Does working at home really work?	Advantages	Disadvantages
The workplace	13	10
The working day	12	8
Commuting	5	3
Technology	11	15
Efficiency	2	9
Costs	7	6
Motivation	16	14
Family	4	1

6 Correspondence

Dialogue (p32, ex6)

A: S-A-G, can I help you?

B: Yes, this is Elena Moretti from Stern Hydraulics. Could I speak to John Bird, please?

A: Oh, hello, Elena. I'm afraid John isn't here at the moment. Can I take a message?

B: Yes, he sent me an order confirmation – the reference is DH010601 – but the delivery date is wrong.

A: Oh, dear. Can you give me the details?

B: Yes, it says July the 7th, but the agreed delivery date was June the 22nd. It's really important.

A: I see. Well, I'll tell him as soon as he comes in.

B: Thank you. I'm not at all happy about this. A lot depends on this order.

A: Right, Elena, leave it with me. I'm terribly sorry about this.

B: No, it's not your fault. Just ask John to phone me.

A: All right, then. Bye for now.

B: Goodbye.

2 Women in business

Fluency (p12, ex7)

Speaker A

Your partner has the missing information. Complete the chart by asking questions like the ones in exercise 6 on page 12.

Name	Janice	Della
Job title		Director of Retail Sales
Type of company		chain of clothing stores
Working hours		45
Responsibilities		Leading a team of 25. Accounts and stock control. Maintaining inventory in stores.
Weekend/Late evening work		One evening and one weekend day a week. Sometimes 'on call' with a pager in case of emergencies.
Most enjoys		Satisfying internal clients. People she works with.
Travel		Not often. Trips to different stores. 3 trade fairs a year.
Holidays		2 weeks. 3 weeks after 5 years' service.
Ratio of women to men in position/field		60% male, 40% female

3 Telephone talk

Roleplay (p19, ex2)

Speaker A

Situation 1

You work as the Publications Officer in the marketing department of Miki-chan Fashion Accessories. You are currently producing your new company brochure. This is a 32-page, full colour brochure on high quality paper. You need 30,000 copies. Phone ADH Graphics for an estimate. The only problem is that the brochure needs to be ready in ten days. Can they do it?

Situation 2

You work for ADH Graphics. A potential client phones you. Listen to what the customer wants and complete the phone contact form below with the necessary information.

Phone Contact Form ADH Graphics

Date:
Call initiated by:
Call handler:

Client:

Address:

Contact:

Position:

Tel:

E-mail:

Nature of business:

Purpose of call:

Comments:

Action required:
By whom:
Date and time:

5 Company histories

Answers: Grammar link (p101, Practice 4)

a Bill Gates didn't found Oracle, he founded Microsoft.
b The Wall Street Crash didn't start a worldwide economic boom, it started an economic depression.
c The six European states didn't sign the Treaty of Madrid, they signed the Treaty of Rome.
d The eleven member states of the European Union didn't adopt the pound as a common currency, they adopted the euro.
e Henry Ford didn't manufacture the first mass produced electronic components, he manufactured cars.
f Napster didn't have problems over people downloading books, it had problems over music.

Answers: Lexis link (p101, Business verbs)

a become
b launch
c expand
d produce
e found
f establish
g achieve
h negotiate
i buy
j provide
k increase

14 Hiring and firing

What about the workers? (p66, ex2)

Student A

1 Read the article, then answer the questions.
2 Find and underline in the article five examples of the passive.
3 Match the five words and phrases in **bold** in the article to five of the definitions below. Ask your partner which words match the other five definitions.

- compensate for _____
- percentage of working population without jobs _____
- employees with training and abilities to do technical tasks _____
- people who are unemployed for a long time _____
- what employees can legally expect from their employers _____
- motivating factors _____
- money paid to people who don't have jobs _____
- all the people who work in a country or for a company _____
- the number of employees a company requires to do its work _____
- workers who have contracts limited to a period of time _____

4 Which country do you think the article is about? Could it be your country? Why? Why not? Explain your reasons to your partner.

Skills shortage linked to job insecurity

According to a survey which was carried out by the Confederation of Industry, almost two thirds of the country's companies are experiencing a shortage of **skilled workers**. It is a problem which particularly affects the electronics industry.

The companies claimed that they provided training for their **workforce**, but that this on its own was not sufficient to cover their **staffing needs**.

In an attempt to **make up for** this lack of skilled workers, nearly half of the 670 firms which were contacted said that they had increased their use of **temporary staff**, and over a quarter intended to do the same in the next year.

According to a spokesman for the Confederation, a result of this skills shortage is an increase in feelings of job insecurity among a third of employees. 'It is increasingly difficult to provide people with jobs for life,' he said.

Although over 60% of firms said staff were paid based on their skills and level of competence, the Confederation noted that while salaries at management level were frequently negotiated individually, conditions for clerical and manual workers were usually agreed at a company-wide level.

6 Correspondence

Answers: Lexis link (p103, crossword)

Across
1. delivery
6. prompt
8. informal
9. handwriting
10. fax
13. business
15. correspondence
19. check
21. decision
22. message
24. annoyed
28. welcome
29. down
30. confirm

Down
2. immediately
3. expensive
4. signature
5. details
7. courier
11. apologise
12. reply
14. Internet
16. worried
17. phoning
18. mistake
20. that
23. skills
25. order
26. send
27. cost

7 Making comparisons

Answers: Road test (p35, ex1)

- The Chevrolet has a **bigger** motor **than** the Maserati.
- The Maserati is **more powerful than** the Chevrolet.
- The Maserati is **faster than** the Chevrolet.
- The Chevrolet is **more economical** (to run) **than** the Maserati.
- The Chevrolet is **longer than** the Maserati.
- The Chevrolet is **wider than** the Maserati.
- The Maserati is **higher than** the Chevrolet.
- The Chevrolet has a **bigger** boot **than** the Maserati.
- The Maserati has a **bigger** fuel tank **than** the Chevrolet.
- The Maserati is **heavier than** the Chevrolet.
- The Maserati/Chevrolet is/looks **better than** the Chevrolet/Maserati. (*your own opinion*)
- The Maserati/Chevrolet is/looks **more attractive than** the Chevrolet/Maserati. (*your own opinion*)
- The Maserati/Chevrolet is/looks **more stylish than** the Chevrolet/Maserati. (*your own opinion*)
- The Maserati/Chevrolet is/looks **sexier than** the Chevrolet/Maserati. (*your own opinion*)

Room service (p37, ex3)

Speaker A
Phone room service to make requests for:
- a bottle of Glenfiddich whisky
- someone to fix the minibar
- someone to explain how the TV pay channels work
- someone to sew on a button
- an extra set of clean towels
- (*your own request*)

9 Spirit of enterprise

The worm man (p41, ex7)

THE WORM MAN

Picture the scene. You go to your bank manager and ask him for money to develop a great business idea – a worm farm. Not surprisingly, the bank manager finds it difficult to keep a straight face. But this isn't an imaginary tale. It's the true story of a business success ...

Let's begin at the beginning. Four years ago, Simon Taylor acquired some land on his family's farm. The river Trent was very near, so at first he thought about fish farming. He rejected the idea. 'The initial investment required was very high, and I'm not the world's biggest risk-taker.'

So, he opted for a worm farm. The start-up costs were low, and Simon began by growing worms and packing them for fishermen into pots ranging in size from 25g to several kilos.

Traditionally, worms eat organic waste in soil, but Simon feeds them salad waste from supermarkets and restaurants. Demand for the worms has grown, so he is looking at the possibilities of using different types of worm food, including toxic waste from the paper industry. When the worms digest the waste, it breaks down into less harmful elements which can be recycled, rather than buried in expensive waste dumps.

'Worms can do things that greatly benefit our environment,' says Simon. This year, the Newark entrepreneur has produced over ten tons of worms, but expects to double production to some twenty tons next year. 'UK fishermen use some 250 tons of worms every year, so there is a healthy demand for a variety of worms already. But we're also looking at using worms in other areas.'

Adapted from The Worm Man by Lee Stokes

9 Spirit of enterprise

Answers: Grammar link (p107, Practice 5)

The Inditex group consists of almost a hundred companies dealing with textile design, production and distribution. Its unique management techniques and its successes (a) **have turned** Inditex into one of the world's largest fashion groups.

Over the years the group (b) **has added** other chains to the original Zara, each covering a different market sector. In 1991 the group (c) **created** Pull & Bear, and in 1995 (d) **acquired** 100% of Massimo Dutti. Bershka (e) **commenced** its activity in 1998, followed by the acquisition of Stradivarius in 1999. More recently, Inditex (f) **launched** Oysho, a chain specialised in fashionable lingerie and underwear.

In the last four years the number of shops in the group (g) **has reached** a figure of over a thousand, and the group now has operations in 39 countries worldwide. In the same period, sales (h) **have increased** by 27% and net profits by 31%. In May 2001 the group was floated on the Madrid stock exchange and its share price (i) **has gone** from strength to strength.

Despite its size, the group still controls its activities from Arteixo, a village in the north west of Spain, where this year it (j) **installed** its headquarters in a new building.

Adapted from www.inditex.com

10 Stressed to the limit

The ten most stressful jobs (p44, ex4)

Measured by level of 21 specific job demands, in the USA the ten most stressful jobs are:

1. Inner-city high school teacher
2. Police officer
3. Miner
4. Air traffic controller
5. Hospital doctor
6. Stockbroker
7. Journalist
8. Customer complaint worker
9. Waiter
10. Secretary

13 Air travel

The negotiation game (p61, ex2)

Speaker A: Buyer

Negotiate with your partner to get the best deal possible. You get points for each category of the deal – price, quantity, delivery time, and so on. For example, if you agree on a price of 6 euros, you get 2 points, or 3 points if the price is 5.5. Add your points for each category to get your score. To be a successful negotiator you have to get at least ten points.

Points	1	2	3	
Price	6.5	6	5.5	€
Quantity	200	150	100	units
Delivery	3	2	1	weeks
Payment	30	60	90	days
Guarantee	6	12	18	months

Useful language

Let's talk about (*price*).
That's my best offer.
Okay, I can go with that.
It's a deal!
I can't go any higher/lower.
I can't do that.
Can you help me on this?

15 Time

Time management (p69, ex7)

The busy manager

His life is not planned. Perhaps that is why he is **busy**. His use of time indicates an entirely responsive approach to his job, with more time devoted to **administration** than customer service. The high level of **emergency** shows there are serious problems.

The effective manager

She **delegates** correspondence to subordinates and deals with major issues herself or by telephone. Her **meetings** are well planned. She is popular with customers and **suppliers** because she gets to know them well and her reading makes her knowledgeable. She doesn't just discuss **problems**; she solves them.

2 Women in business

Fluency (p12, ex7)

Speaker B

Your partner has the missing information. Complete the chart by asking questions like the ones in exercise 6 on page 12.

Name	Janice	Della
Job title	Production Manager	
Type of company	software company	
Working hours	Normally 40-50 hours but can be up to 75.	
Responsibilities	Managing website. Liasing with international offices.	
Weekend/Late evening work	Not in her present position.	
Most enjoys	Doing something that makes a real difference to the company.	
Travel	Occasional trips to other offices.	
Holidays	3 weeks	
Ratio of women to men in position/field	Half the department are women but only two have technical skills.	

3 Telephone talk

Roleplay (p19, ex2)

Speaker B

Situation 1

You work for ADH Graphics. A potential client phones you. Listen to what the customer wants and complete the phone contact form below with the necessary information.

Situation 2

You work as the Marketing Manager in the marketing department of a clothes manufacturer, Lewis & Co. You are looking for someone to print some labels for your new range of jeans. The labels have to be printed on quality card in two colours. They also have to be cut to the shape of the company logo. You want 10,000 labels. Phone ADH Graphics for an estimate.

Phone Contact Form ADH Graphics

Date:
Call initiated by:
Call handler:

Client:

Address:

Contact:

Position:

Tel:

E-mail:

Nature of business:

Purpose of call:

Comments:

Action required:
By whom:
Date and time:

6 Correspondence

Answers: On-the-spot decisions (p30, ex5)

Problems	Solutions
I've got a headache.	I'll get you an aspirin.
I can't understand these figures.	I'll explain them to you.
My computer keeps crashing.	I'll call the IT technician.
We didn't get your fax.	I'll send it to you again.
This report has lots of errors in it.	I'll go through it and correct them.
I can't remember his phone number.	I'll look it up for you.
I need to speak to you urgently.	I'll phone you this afternoon.
I haven't booked my flight to Berlin.	I'll reserve the tickets for you this morning.
The printer is not working properly.	I'll change the ink cartridge.
I don't know how to use this program.	I'll show you how it works.
I need three copies of this proposal.	I'll print them out for you.
I don't know anything about this company.	I'll look for information on the Internet.
Our e-mail system isn't working.	I'll fax the details to you instead.
I can't get an answer from the taxi service.	I'll take you to the airport.

7 Making comparisons

World leaders (p36, ex1)

Speaker B

Look at the tables below. Your partner has the missing information. Ask questions to complete the tables. For example, *Which is **the second biggest** hotel chain / car manufacturer in the world? Where is it based? How many rooms does it have / cars does it sell?*

The six biggest hotel chains ranked by number of rooms		Company	Country	Number of rooms
	1	_____	_____	_____
	2	Bass Hotels & Resorts	UK	471,680
	3	Marriott International	_____	355,900
	4	_____	_____	_____
	5	Choice Hotels	USA	338,254
	6	Best Western	USA	_____
Top six car manufacturers in the world ranked by sales		Company	Country	Sales (in millions)
	1	General Motors	USA	6.60
	2	_____	_____	_____
	3	VW Group	Germany	_____
	4	Toyota	Japan	3.87
	5	Daimler Chrysler	_____	2.83
	6	_____	_____	_____

6 Correspondence

On-the-spot decisions (p30, ex5)

Speaker B

Speaker A will begin by telling you a problem. Offer a solution from the table. Say *Don't worry, I'll ...*
Then tell Speaker A about a problem from the table. Begin *I've got a problem ...* Speaker A will offer a solution.

For example: **A** I've got a problem, the battery in my mobile's flat.   **B** Don't worry, I'll lend you mine.

Problems	Solutions
I can't understand these figures.	... look it up for you.
My computer keeps crashing.	... look for information on the Internet.
I need to speak to you urgently.	... reserve the tickets for you this morning.
The printer is not working properly.	... send it to you again.
I don't know how to use this program.	... get you an aspirin.
Our e-mail system isn't working.	... go through it and correct them.
I can't get an answer from the taxi service.	... print them out for you.

Answers on page 131

Fluency (page 32, ex8)

Speaker B

You are John Bird. You understand why Elena Moretti is angry. Her company is one of your best customers. Your production department let you down. They promised to meet the delivery date but there was a transport strike and some components didn't arrive. Apologise as much as you can for what happened and invent excuses for everything. Offer to pay for a holiday weekend in London for Elena and but don't make any promises you can't keep.

---

13 Air travel

The negotiation game (p61, ex2)

Speaker B: Seller
Negotiate with your partner to get the best deal possible. You get points for each category of the deal – price, quantity, delivery time, and so on. For example, if you agree on a price of 6 euros, you get 2 points, or 3 points if the price is 6.5. Add your points for each category to get your score. To be a successful negotiator you have to get at least ten points.

Points	1	2	3	
Price	5.5	6	6.5	€
Quantity	100	150	200	units
Delivery	1	2	3	weeks
Payment	90	60	30	days
Guarantee	18	12	6	months

Useful language

Let's talk about (*price*).
That's my best offer.
Okay, I can go with that.
It's a deal!
I can't go any higher/lower.
I can't do that.
Can you help me on this?

3 Telephone talk

Could you tell me ...? (p19, ex4)

Speaker B
You were just about to send this e-mail to a colleague, when they ring you. Answer their questions.

> To:
> From:
> Subject: Annual sales meeting
> You're on flight BA 44362 at 1955 on the 21st December from London Heathrow terminal 2. You'll be met by a taxi which will take you to the factory to meet Mr Fuentes. It's about 40 kilometres from the airport. You've got one hour with Mr Fuentes. Then you leave to get to the hotel for the meeting. You'll need to go across country. Avis have either a Range Rover 3.6 or Jeep Grand Cherokee, whichever you prefer. An armed guide will accompany you. Don't forget that you'll need to carry your passport and international driving licence at all times.
> The hotel is The Lodge. It's in the middle of the forest, twenty miles from the nearest town, and has 5 stars. All the rooms (including the meeting room) have been booked for the whole week.
> All the best,

9 Spirit of enterprise

Change (p42, ex4)

Speaker B
Look at the information in the table. Work with your partner to complete the missing information and find out how Inditex has changed over the last four years.

Inditex	four years ago	now
Shops worldwide	748	
Shops in Spain	489	
Shops in rest of world	259	
Countries where the group operates	21	
Chains in group	Zara, Pull & Bear, Massimo Dutti	
Net revenues	€1,615 million	
Net profits	€153 million	
Headquarters	Arteixo, La Coruña, Spain	

14 Hiring and firing

What about the workers? (p66, ex2)

Student B
1. Read the article, then answer the questions.
2. Find and underline in the article five examples of the passive.
3. Match the five words and phrases in **bold** in the article to five of the definitions below. Ask your partner which words match the other five definitions.
   - compensate for _____
   - percentage of working population without jobs _____
   - employees with training and abilities to do technical tasks _____
   - people who are unemployed for a long time _____
   - what employees can legally expect from their employers _____
   - motivating factors _____
   - money paid to people who don't have jobs _____
   - all the people who work in a country or for a company _____
   - the number of employees a company requires to do its work _____
   - workers who have contracts limited to a period of time _____
4. Which country do you think the article is about? Could it be your country? Why? Why not? Explain your reasons to your partner.

17 Office gossip

Gossip (p80, ex9)

Speaker B
You are the personnel manager of the company with the notice below about coffee breaks. You think a lot of time is wasted by people chatting and gossiping when they are supposed to be working. You are under pressure from the Managing Director to improve the efficiency of the company. Also, recently there have been a lot of rumours about staff cutbacks. Most of them are false but some are true, and this is creating a lot of problems.

COMPANY NOTICE

Employees may take up to three coffee breaks per day.

Maximum time at coffee machine: four minutes.

All 'gossip' or discussion of non-work related matters is prohibited.

Unions general strike threat

The whole of the country will be brought to a halt if plans for a general strike go ahead. The threatened strike has been called by the unions in reaction to the government's attempts to cut **unemployment benefits**. With the proposed changes unemployed workers will have to take one of the first three 'acceptable' job offers which are put to them, if the place of work is within 30 km of their homes. If they refuse, they will lose their benefits. Also, anyone who is sacked from their job but appealing against the decision will lose their salary entitlement during the period of the appeal.

The two main unions, each with over a million members each, say that the reforms are a direct attack on **workers' rights**. They say the changes will be especially negative for those who lose their jobs, and the **long-term unemployed**. They also claim that the new law will make it easier and cheaper for companies to lay off staff, and will lead to increased job insecurity.

With an 11.3% **unemployment rate**, the highest in the European Union, the reforms have been defended by the government, which says they are necessary in order to be competitive and provide an open and flexible labour market. It says the measures will help solve the problem of unemployment by increasing the **incentives** for people to find jobs. Although its relations with the labour movement have been generally good for the last six years, trade union officials say that this time the government has gone too far.

Recordings

1 Selling your company

1.1

Hello, my name is Nick Jenkins, and the name of my company is Moonpig. We operate a website that allows users to select and personalise greetings cards, which we print and post within 24 hours. Customers can choose from more than 650 cards and can customise the captions on the cover as well as the greeting.
I have an MBA and previous experience setting up sugar and grain trading operations in the former Soviet Union. I employ 12 people at Moonpig.
Our competitive advantage is that this is one of the few times that you can buy something from the Internet that's actually better than a similar product that you can buy in a shop. We have a £750,000 digital printing system that allows us to print and laminate cards. Our running costs are low and we are making a profit of £1.20 on each card sold, which is a margin of 60%.
Our potential market is enormous. 92% of the British population buy an average of 12 cards each a year. The greetings card business is worth more than £1 billion a year in the UK and £10 billion worldwide. We're very successful. At the moment we have 15,000 registered users. Our turnover is increasing by 50% a month and we are expecting to be profitable within six months. Our target is to get 300,000 customers in the UK and 750,000 worldwide in five years.
We are looking for between two million and three million pounds of investment to finance marketing in the UK and the US. Our direct mail campaigns are proving particularly successful, and I am talking to venture capitalists in the US about setting up a website there.

2 Women in business

2.1

A: Oh, look, here's something in our field.
B: **What's the position?**
A: Design Team Co-ordinator.
B: Yes, but **what kind of company is it?**
A: They produce computer games software.
B: So, **what does the job involve, then?**
A: Well, her name's Joanne, and she says that she's responsible for anything design-related in the company. And that it's very rewarding.
B: **What does she most enjoy about the work?**
A: She has a huge amount of responsibility, opportunities to learn, and it never gets boring because the job is always changing.
B: **How many hours a week does she work?**
A: Up to sixty hours a week.
B: Sixty hours a week!
A: Yes, eleven hours on weekdays and a half-day over the weekend.
B: That's sounds an awful lot.
A: Yes, but hang on. That's only during development stages. It's usually forty to forty-five hours.
B: **Does she have to work evenings?**
A: It doesn't say. She doesn't start that early, though. Most days she gets in at around nine thirty, it says.
B: **What's the ratio of women to men in this job?**
A: Let's see. Three out of the fourteen in her company are women, which she says is unusually balanced for the computer games industry.
B: Balanced! Why?
A: Because on the whole these companies only employ women as decoration for their stands at conferences.
B: Well, that doesn't sound very positive. **How much travel does she get?**
A: None at all. She never travels because she can do everything from the office. Travelling is for holidays.
B: And **how much holiday do they give her?**
A: Five weeks a year. Sounds quite generous.
B: Yes, it's more than most companies offer.
A: Hmm. It's just the kind of job I'm looking for. I wonder how she got into it.
B: Be assertive without being rude and stick up for yourself when you're right. That's her advice.

3 Telephone talk

3.1

1
Twenty-five per cent.

2
Six hundred and thirty-two thousand, two hundred and thirty-three.

3
Two million dollars.

4
Four point three million pounds.

5
Six euros twenty-five.

6
Five point six two three four.

7
Three thousand and twenty-two pounds.

8
Six million, five hundred and seventy-six thousand, three hundred and fifty-eight.

9
Two plus two equals four.

10
Eight minus two equals six.

11
Five times three equals fifteen.

12
Twelve divided by three equals four.

3.2

A: InterAir, can I help you?
B: Yes, please. I'd like some information about a flight arriving from Munich.
A: Yes. **Do you know what the flight number is?**
B: The flight number? I'm not sure. I know it leaves Munich at 1730.
A: Oh, yes, that's IA 345.
B: Yes, that's it. **Could you tell me what time it gets in?**
A: Yes, the arrival time is 1910.
B: 1910. **Do you know if there's any delay?**
A: No, the flight is on time.
B: Right, thank you very much.
A: You're welcome. Goodbye.

3.3

A: Hello, could I speak to Mr White, please?
B: Speaking. How can I help you?
A: Hello, Mr White. My name is Clarkson, from Bellstone & Smith, the elevator manufacturers.
B: Yes, I think I've heard of you.
A: I'm in charge of the customer support department. I'm phoning to ask for an estimate. It's for a service manual we're preparing.
B: Oh, yes. I don't think we've done anything for you before.
A: No, that's right. We're in the process of updating all our manuals. If the price is right, it will mean quite a lot of work.
B: I see. Well, could you give me the details, then?
A: Yes, it's for a manual of just over 100 pages.
B: 100 pages. Could you tell me what size?
A: It's in A5. We want to print 20,000. But I'd like estimates for 10,000 and 30,000 as well.
B: I see. Is it in colour?
A: No, it's in black and white. Mainly text. The cover is in colour, though. I can put it all on a CD for you. Is that all right?
B: Yes, that would be perfect. Could I just read my notes back?

A: Yes, go ahead.
B: You want quotes for print runs of 10,000, 20,000 and 30,000 of an A5 100-page manual in black and white. The cover is in colour and you'll be presenting the material on disk or CD.
A: That's right.
B: Would you like me to visit you with some samples?
A: Yes, okay.
B: Would tomorrow morning suit you?
A: No, I'm out of the office tomorrow. How about Friday? About ten o'clock?
B: Friday ... the 16th ... at ten. That's fine. I'll bring the estimates with me and we can discuss the details then.
A: Fine.
B: Oh, could you give me the address?
A: Yes, it's 14, Clapham Road, London SW14.
B: And your telephone number?
A: 0207 839 4216.
B: 0207 839 4216. Right. Oh, do you have e-mail?
A: Yes, it's clarkson.bellstone@lineone.com.
B: Can I just check that? clarkson, dot, bellstone at lineone, dot, com.
A: Okay, then, Mr White. See you on Friday.
B: Yes. Goodbye, then.
A: Goodbye.

4 Networking

4.1
Conversation 1
A: Hello, **do you mind if I join you?**
B: Er, no, not at all.
A: How do you do? My name's Rick Van Looy.
B: Hi. Pleased to meet you. I'm Florent Rondele.
A: **Are you from around here, then?**
B: No, but my company has a store in town. Actually, I live in France.
A: So, **what do you do**, Florent?
B: I'm in marketing. I work for a retail company. We deal mainly in leisure goods.
A: **Do you mean sports equipment?**
B: Well, both sports and casual wear. Clothes, shoes, accessories, stuff like that. We have stores in several countries.
A: Sounds like a big operation. How many stores have you got?
B: Nearly fifty in total. And **what line of business are you in, Rick?**
A: Well, quite similar really. I'm a sales manager for a large Dutch clothing firm, Verweij Fashion – do you know it?
B: Yes, of course. Are you opening a store here, then?
A: Yes, we're looking at possible sites at the moment.
B: Hm. That can be a slow process. Rick, **do you fancy something to drink?**
A: Erm, yeah, thanks.
B: Come on, then. **There's a table free over there.**

Conversation 2
A: Excuse me, does this belong to you?
B: Oh, thank you very much.
A: It was on the floor.
B: Yes, I was looking for it just now. I wanted to finish this crossword. I'm feeling a bit groggy, actually.
A: Yes, it's a long flight.
B: Oh, isn't it? **Have you got the time?**
A: Yes, it's ... erm ... just after midnight.
B: So, do we land soon?
A: Yes, in about half an hour.
B: Oh, good. **Do you know Bangkok?**
A: Yes, I live there. **Is this your first trip there?**
B: Yes, it is actually.
A: On business, I suppose?
B: Yes, I'm visiting a supplier.
A: Oh, really? I wonder if I ...

4.2
A: **Do you know Jan Nowacki?**
B: Yes, isn't he Director of Business Development at Guinness?
A: Not any longer. Now he's the Public Relations Manager at the National Bank of Poland.
B: The National Bank of Poland, that's interesting. **Do you have any contact with him in your work?**
A: Not really, but I occasionally play golf with him.
B: **What's he like?**
A: He's a nice chap. You'd like him.

5 Company histories

5.1
The Japanese company, Nintendo, is the world leader in interactive entertainment systems. To date, Nintendo has sold more than one billion video games worldwide, including Nintendo 64 and GameBoy, the world's best-selling video game.
The history of Nintendo goes back to 1902, when Fusajiro Yamauchi, the great grandfather of the present day president, **manufactured** the first playing cards in Japan. Although they were originally for export, the cards became popular in Japan as well as abroad.
Yamauchi **founded** an unlimited partnership, Yamauchi Nintendo & Company, in 1933. Thirty years later, in 1963, the company **changed** its name to Nintendo Co. Ltd., and started to manufacture games in addition to playing cards.
In 1970 Nintendo **reconstructed** and **enlarged** its corporate headquarters, and introduced electronic technology into its products. It **developed** the first video game in 1975, and the following year **used** a microprocessor in a game system for the first time.
A key year in the company's history was 1980, when Nintendo **established** a subsidiary in the USA, Nintendo of America, Inc. Five years passed before it **started** sales in the States of NES, the Nintendo Entertainment System, which **reached** number one selling toy status in just two years.
Perhaps the most significant event in Nintendo's recent history was in 1989 when it **introduced** the first portable hand-held game system with interchangeable game packs, GameBoy. GameBoy was a tremendous success and in 1995 the company **celebrated** the sales of its one billionth game pack.
When Nintendo **launched** Nintendo 64 in Japan on June 23 1996, it sold more than 500,000 units on the first day. Two years later it **released** Pokemon, a breakthrough game concept for GameBoy which generated a worldwide craze and, in 1999, the company **expanded** the Pokemon franchise, which was by then an international social phenomenon. GameBoy Advanced, which introduced improvements and additional features to the original GameBoy, hit the market in 2001, continuing Nintendo's commitment to constant innovation and quality in its game systems.

5.2
Was the Internet born in 1969 or in 1983? It all depends on who you talk to.
In 1965, the Advanced Research Projects Agency under the US Department of Defense, **began** work on a system to connect computers. They **called** the project ARPANET.
On September 2nd, 1969, Professor Leonard Kleinrock connected the first two machines. Twenty people **watched** in a laboratory at the University of California as meaningless data flowed between two computers along a 15 foot grey cable. For many people, that day **marked** the birth of today's Internet.
The next month they sent the first message on the Net to a computer at Stanford University. The message was 'lo'. They **wanted** to send the words 'log in' but when they typed 'g' the system **crashed**. In fact the first word was quite appropriate, as a phonetic version of 'hello'.
By January 1970 ARPANET **linked** computers in four American universities, and by the following year there were 23 hosts in the system, connecting different universities and research institutes.
In 1973 Ray Tomlinson **sent** the first e-mail via ARPANET. In the same year it also went international, connecting hosts in England and Norway.
Another landmark was in 1979 when two graduate students at Duke University **established** the first USENET newsgroups. Users from all over the world **joined** these discussion groups to talk about the Net, politics, religion and thousands of other subjects.
In 1974 Bob Kahn and Vincent Cerf **invented** a software that allowed ARPANET to connect to other networks using different operating systems. The software, called TCP/IP, **became** the universal language of the Internet on January 1st, 1983. Some people say that this was the true birth of the Net.
More and more networks joined the system and the number of hosts **increased** dramatically: from 10,000 in 1984 to 100,000 in 1987.

By the early 1990s the World Wide Web was the most popular way of browsing the web, and the network was accessible to anyone in the world with a computer. In 1992 the number of hosts **reached** 1,000,000.

In 1993, Mosaic **became** available. This was the first graphics-based browser of the type we all use today. The growth rate of the Internet was an incredible 341% and by 1998 there were over 30,000,000 hosts.

6 Correspondence

6.1

A: JFA Fabrics, can I help you?
B: Yes, I'm phoning from Natural Furnishings in Chelsea. Could I speak to Peter Simpson, please?
A: I'm afraid he's out of the office right now. Can I help you?
B: Well, it's about a fax I sent him. I'm waiting for a reply and it's quite urgent.
A: What's it about exactly?
B: It's a bit complicated to explain on the phone. I need a copy of a certificate for customs. Maybe he didn't get my fax. Can I just check your fax number – 0208 530 6370?
A: Yes, that's right. Listen, **why don't you send the details to me by e-mail and I'll send you a copy of the certificate** as an attached Acrobat file.
B: Yes, that's a good idea. What's your e-mail address?
A: Jim, dot. That's J-I-M, dot, J-F-A, at lineone, dot, net. Lineone is all one word.
B: Can I just check that? Jim, dot, JFA, at lineone, dot, net.
A: Yes, that's right.
B: Okay, **I'll deal with the e-mail straight away**. By the way, my name's Cathy, Cathy Slater. You must be Jim.
A: Yes, Jim Kutz. Don't worry about the certificate. You'll have it by this afternoon.
B: Okay, thanks for your help.
A: You're welcome. Bye.

6.2

A: Have we got a decision from Jim about the Mason contract?
B: No, don't worry. **I'll call him about it this afternoon**.
A: I tried – there's no answer.
B: Well, **I'll send him an e-mail**, then.
A: You can't – our intranet is down.
B: Never mind – **I'll send him a fax**.
A: I don't think we have their fax number.
B: Well, in that case, **I'll write him a letter** before I leave the office.
A: Oh, come on, that'll take far too long.
B: So, **we'll have to fly out to see him!**
A: Oh, that's a bit expensive ...

6.3

A: S-A-G, can I help you?
B: Yes, could I speak to John Bird?
A: I'm afraid he's not in the office right now. Can I take a message?
B: Oh, dear! It's an urgent order – we need five hydraulic pumps by June the 22nd.
A: Just a minute. Could you tell me your name, please?
B: Yes, I'm sorry. It's Elena Moretti from Stern Hydraulics in Switzerland.
A: Right, I'll take down the details and get John to contact you. Did you say five units?
B: Yes, the reference is SG 94321.
A: SG 94321 – five units.
B: Yes, that's right. But the important thing is the delivery date – June the 22nd.
A: I don't think that will be a problem.
B: Good, it's for a new customer.
A: I see. Right, when John comes in, I'll tell him immediately. Could you confirm the order in writing?
B: Yes, of course. Thanks very much.
A: You're welcome. Goodbye.
B: Goodbye.

6.4

A: Could I speak to Elena Moretti, please?
B: Speaking. Is that John?
A: Yes. Hello, Elena. I'm phoning back about your order.
B: Yes, it's quite urgent.
A: Don't worry. I've got all the details in your fax. No problem.
B: That's good. I was worried about it.
A: Well, can I help you with anything else?
B: No, but I hope we get more business from this customer.
A: Yes, of course. Okay, I'll be in touch. Bye for now.
B: Goodbye.

6.5

A: S-A-G, can I help you?
B: Yes, this is Elena Moretti from Stern Hydraulics. Could I speak to John Bird, please?
A: Oh, hello, Elena, I'm afraid John isn't here at the moment. Can I take a message?
B: Yes, he sent me an order confirmation – the reference is DH010601 – but the delivery date is wrong.
A: Oh, dear. Can you give me the details?
B: Yes, it says July the 7th, but the agreed delivery date was June the 22nd. It's really important.
A: I see. Well, I'll tell him as soon as he comes in.
B: Thank you. I'm not at all happy about this. A lot depends on this order.
A: Right, Elena, leave it with me. I'm terribly sorry about this.
B: No, it's not your fault. Just ask John to phone me.
A: All right, then. Bye for now.
B: Goodbye.

7 Making comparisons

7.1

A: Good afternoon.
B: Good afternoon. I have a reservation in the name of Wilson.
A: Er ... yes, that's right. Did you have a good flight, sir?
B: Yes, not too bad. It was a bit long.
A: Could I see your passport, please?
B: Yes, of course. Here you are.
A: Thank you, your room is 301. Would you like some breakfast sent up to your room?
B: Breakfast? Em ... yes, that would be nice.
A: Would you like tea or coffee?
B: Coffee, please. Oh, em, I need to send an e-mail.
A: That's no problem. You'll find a terminal in your room.
B: Right, thanks.
A: You're welcome. Have a good stay.

7.2

A: Room service. My name is Johan. Can I help you?
B: Yes, this is room 301. Could I have an early morning call, please?
A: Certainly, sir. What time would you like the call?
B: At half past six.
A: 6.30. No problem. Would you like breakfast sent up to your room?
B: No, thanks. I'll have it in the dining room.
A: The dining room opens for breakfast at 7.30.
B: Oh, in that case I will have it in my room. Just coffee and a croissant.
A: Coffee and a croissant. Anything else?
B: No, that's all.
A: Okay. Good night, sir.
B: Thank you. Good night.

8 Did I ever tell you ...?

8.1

A: Look at that car!
B: Yes, it's a real beauty. Porsche 911.
A: Did I ever tell you about the time I had a ride in a Porsche?
B: No, I don't think so.
A: **It was when I was a student. I was hitch-hiking in Europe** and this chap in a Porsche stopped. He took me all the way across Austria. We went about 220 kilometres an hour all the way.
B: What about the police?
A: Well, they stopped us about four times, but this chap just showed some identity card and they waved us on.
B: Was he someone important, then?
A: I don't know, I didn't ask. I suppose he was some sort of high-ranking official. **He didn't talk much, but we *did* get there very quickly.**

8.2

a
Yes, that was a long time ago. **It was while I was living in Italy.** I had this apartment in the centre of Milan ...

b
I can remember what happened. **It was before I started working here.** I was working on a temporary basis ...

c
No, it wasn't until much later. **It was after I left university.** I'd got my degree ...

d
Oh, yes, that reminds me. **It was when I was working at ICL.** I was in the marketing department ...

e
I had more time in those days. **It was before I got married.** In fact, I hadn't even met Mary ...

f
The timing was awful. **It was just after my children were born.** And there I was without ...

g
I'd just arrived in London. **I was looking for a job.** I bought the paper every day ...

h
Yes, I was still studying at the time. **I was doing my Masters in the States.** At the Harvard Business School, in fact ...

i
I was nineteen. **I was studying at Cambridge.** Things weren't going very well ...

j
No, it was with a different set-up. **I was working for a small company north of here.** One day the boss walked into ...

k
I was having a gap year after university. **I was travelling through Asia.** I'd just arrived in Saigon and ...

l
It happened last March. **I was staying at the Continental Hotel in Prague.** Lovely hotel, I recommend it.

8.3

a
We had a good time but it *did* cost a fortune!

b
He got the job but he *did* have to marry the boss' daughter!

c
We got there in the end but we *did* sit on a bus all day.

d
I got a good job but I *did* have to leave the country to find one.

e
She made a success of her business but her husband *did* leave her.

f
He sold more than anyone else but he *did* have a heart attack.

9 Spirit of enterprise

9.1

A: Good morning. Please sit down.
B: Good morning. Thank you for seeing me.
A: Let's see, then. How can I help you, Simon?
B: Well, I'd like to borrow some money to set up a business.
A: What kind of business were you thinking of?
B: Well, em, I know it sounds strange, but I have this idea for setting up a worm farm.
A: A what?
B: A worm farm ... a farm to produce worms for fishing bait.
A: Is there really a market for it?
B: Yes, but apart from fishing bait, worms can recycle food waste.
A: I see.
B: And, in Holland, they use worms to produce a special kind of soil which is ideal for growing organic tomatoes.
A: Well, could I see your business plan ...?

9.2

A: Simon, where did you get the idea for a worm farm?
B: Well, my family owns a farm, and some of the land wasn't being used.
A: So, you had the land available. Was this your first idea for a business?
B: No, at first I thought of fish farming or maggots for fishermen.
A: Why did you change your mind?
B: I decided the investment was too big. I didn't want to take a risk.
A: So, why did you decide to set up a worm farm?
B: Because the start-up costs were relatively low.
A: How did you start, then?
B: I began by packing worms in pots for fishermen.
A: What do you feed them?
B: I mainly feed them salad waste from supermarkets and restaurants, but as demand has grown, we've tried other food sources.
A: For example?
B: Well, we've fed them with toxic waste from the paper industry.
A: Really? Does it work?
B: Yes, the results have been very positive. They can recycle the waste. It's cheaper than burying it in expensive dumps. And it's good for the environment.
A: It sounds amazing. How much do you produce?
B: This year we've produced ten tons of worms, and next year we hope to double production to twenty.
A: There's a market for all these worms, then.
B: Oh, yes. In the UK, fisherman use around 250 tons of worms every year, so there's a healthy demand. But we're also looking at other uses.
A: Well, Simon, that's all very interesting. Thanks very much and good luck for the future.
B: Thank you. You're welcome.

10 Stressed to the limit

10.1

Interview 1
A: According to statistics, around 75% of all visits to the doctor are the result of work-related stress. Do you think you suffer from stress? That's the question we're asking in the streets of Edinburgh. Excuse me, I'm from the radio programme *Work Today*. We're doing a survey on stress. Would you mind answering some questions?
B: Eh, well, actually, I'm in a bit of a hurry, but ... em ... go on, then.
A: Thank you. What's your job?
B: I'm an accountant.
A: Do you suffer from stress in your work?
B: Eh, yes, I do, I think.
A: What symptoms do you notice?
B: Em, I get a lot of headaches and I sleep very badly.
A: And what causes your stress?
B: It's my boss. He's a real ... well, let's just say he doesn't exactly make life easy. He always wants things done for yesterday.
A: Thank you very much.

Interview 2
A: ... and what do you do?
C: I work in a shop.
A: Do you suffer from stress?
C: No, not at work, I don't. I find being at home more stressful.
A: Why's that?
C: Well, I've got three children and my mother's ill. She lives with us. And my husband ... well, he doesn't help much.
A: And do you have any physical symptoms?
C: Well, I get a bit on edge at times and then I get this horrible rash on my neck.
A: So, stress is a problem in your life.
C: Yes, definitely.

Interview 3
A: ... and you, sir. Do you suffer from stress?
D: Well, to tell the truth, I'm off work at the moment because of it.
A: Really, what do you do?
D: I'm a teacher. I work with teenagers and I don't know why but every year they seem to get worse.
A: Yes, that does sound stressful.

D: Everyone thinks teaching's an easy option because of the holidays, but you get to a point where you just can't handle it any longer. You lose control. I almost hit a lad with a spanner, so I went to the doctor and he said it was stress.
A: Well, I hope things get better for you.
D: Thanks, but I think that basically the solution is probably to change jobs. Fortunately, I'm still young enough to do that.
A: Right. Good luck, then.

Interview 4
A: Can I ask you if you suffer from stress?
E: Who? Me? No, not at all. I don't really understand what it is, really.
A: And what do you do for a living?
E: I'm a self-employed architect. I work for myself.
A: I see, and what's your secret?
E: I'm sorry?
A: I mean, how do you avoid getting stressed?
E: I think it's all down to a philosophy of life. I just take each day as it comes. I don't worry about things. What I say is that if you've got a problem, solve it. And if you can't because there's no solution, there's no point in worrying because that won't help.
A: So, you think avoiding stress is to do with mental attitude, not what you do?
E: Yes, that's basically it.
A: Well, thanks very much.
E: Not at all.

11 Top jobs

11.1

Who is the boss of the world's leading manufacturer of personal and business computing software? Ask most people and they will say the mega rich Bill Gates. But no, the planet's wealthiest man stepped down from the top job in January 2000 to take on a new appointment and pursue what he claims is his real passion. Apparently this is not making money, but designing software. **Since then, the chief executive of Microsoft Corporation has been his old university chum, Steve Ballmer.**

History tells us that Gates dropped out of Harvard to set up Microsoft with Paul Allen in 1975. Meanwhile, his other friend Steve, who lived down the hall, graduated with a degree in mathematics and economics. He then went on to work for two years at Proctor and Gamble, and attend the Stanford University Graduate School of Business.

Ballmer has worked for Microsoft since 1980, when Gates remembered his college mate and hired him as the company's first business manager. **Over the last 20 years Ballmer has been in charge of several Microsoft divisions**, including operations, operation system development, and sales and support. In July 1998 he was promoted to president, a role that gave him day-to-day responsibility for running the company. However, **since Gates became 'Chief Software Architect', Ballmer has assumed full management control of Microsoft.** (Just in case, Bill has retained some power as Chairman.)

Legend has it that in spring 1986, soon after hiring Ballmer, Gates called him into his office. Microsoft's deadline to produce Windows was getting behind schedule, and Gates reportedly threatened to fire his friend if the software wasn't on the shelves by the end of the year. Needless to say, Windows was ready by the end of the year, and **they have remained the best of friends.** Proof of this is that Steve was best man at Bill's wedding.

Ballmer has influenced Microsoft with his own brand of energy and discipline. He says, 'I want everyone to share my passion for our products and services. I want people to understand the amazing, positive way our software can make leisure time more enjoyable, and businesses more successful.' Ballmer jogs daily and loves basketball.

 11.2

A: Good morning. Could I speak to Peter Davis, please?
B: Speaking.
A: Oh, hello, Mr Davis. My name is John Lindsay.
B: What can I do for you, Mr Lindsay?
A: It's more a case of what I can do for you ... Em, **how long have you worked for Blueprint International**, Mr Davis?
B: **For about six years.** Why do you ask?
A: And before that you worked for Navigate for three years.
B: Yes, I joined them as a trainee manager when I left university. But ... what is this about?
A: And you were made head of the International Division a year ago. How is it going?
B: Very well, thank you. Now, could you tell me what you want, Mr Lindsay?
A: I'd like to talk to you about an extremely interesting career opportunity. I work for *People Search*, the management consultants. **We've been approached by a client** who is looking for someone with just your professional profile.
B: Oh, I see. So that's what it's about. Listen, Mr Lindsay, I'm really quite busy and ...
A: Yes, I understand that but you should know I'm talking about a considerable salary increase. **You've been married for a couple of years now** and recently became a father, I believe.
B: What's that got to do with it?
A: Well, think about your family and the financial possibilities of an advantageous career move at this moment in your life. I think you should at least talk to me.
B: Em, well, I suppose so. What's the name of the company?
A: I'd rather not say over the phone. Perhaps we could meet to discuss things further?
B: I'm not sure I'm that interested ... **Blueprint International have been very good to me.**
A: Oh, come on, Peter! What are the real prospects in your present post? **You've got as far as you can in Blueprint.** Do you want to be in the same place ten years from now? At least find the time to talk to us.
B: I'd like to think about it. Can I phone you back?
A: No, I'd prefer to phone you back myself in a couple of days. In the meantime, **think about what I've said.** A more stimulating work situation, not to mention a considerable rise in salary ... Talk it over with your wife.
B: Fair enough.
A: Oh, and one more thing, Peter. I'd appreciate it if you didn't mention this call to anyone in your company, okay?
B: Yes, yes, all right. So, you'll call me, then?
A: That's right. In a couple of days. We'll arrange a meeting somewhere. Bye for now, then.
B: Bye.

12 Conversation gambits

12.1

1
A: Excuse me, **are you here for the ITM conference?**
B: Yes, that's right.
A: Me too. Do you know where to register?
B: I think it's over there.
A: Oh, yes. Right, **I'm Paulo, by the way.**
B: Hello, Paulo, I'm Kate. Let's go and register.

2
C: Phew! Is it me, or is it boiling in here?
D: Yes, they always seem to have the heating on full.
C: **So, it's not your first time.**
D: No, it's my fourth time here.
C: Oh, right, **so you're an old hand.** I'm Boris.
D: David. **Pleased to meet you.**

3
E: Is it my mobile phone, or is there some problem with coverage here?
F: Oh, hang on. No, mine seems to be working okay.
E: Typical, flat batteries and nowhere to charge up.
F: **Can I lend you mine?**
E: **Oh, that's very kind**, but I was expecting a call on this number.
F: I see.
E: **My name's Nadine, by the way. From Xanadu Electronics.**
F: Pleased to meet you. I'm Miko.

4
G: Excuse me, **do you know anything about this speaker?**
H: No, I'm sorry, I don't.
G: **I can't find my programme notes.**
H: Oh, here. **Borrow mine.**

G: Thanks. **By the way, I'm Bill Smart from Silicon Technologies.**
H: Right, **how do you do?** I'm Kazuo Yamada from Lexico.

12.2
A: Excuse me. **Would you mind if I had a quick look at your newspaper?**
B: Er, **no, go ahead**. I've finished with it.
A: There's just something I want to check out.
B: **No problem. Take your time.**
A: Thanks. **By the way, my name's Allan. I'm here on a business trip.**
B: Oh, right.

12.3
A: Here's your paper then. Thanks very much.
B: **Don't mention it.**
A: I'm afraid my team didn't win.
B: Sorry?
A: The football results.
B: Oh, I see.
A: **Can I buy you a drink? If you don't have anything else to do, that is.**
B: **I was just about to go, actually**, but ... yes, why not, ... Al, I think you said your name was.
A: Allan, Allan Vilkas.

12.4
B: I'm Sean, Sean O'Malley.
A: **Pleased to meet you, Sean. What would you like to drink?**
B: A beer, please.
A: Right. Two beers, please.
C: Right, sir.
B: **So, Allan, where are you from?**
A: Well, I was born in Lithuania, but I've lived in Germany most of my life. Are you from here?
B: **Yes, what do you think of Dublin?**
A: Well, I've only just arrived today and it's my first visit, but it seems very nice. Lots of character.
B: **Are you here on business?**
A: Yes, that's right. I have a meeting tomorrow. I'm a bit nervous about it.
B I'm sure it'll go all right. **How long are you staying?**
A: **Just a couple of days.** I go back on Thursday morning. I was just looking at your paper to see how Bayern Munich did yesterday. **Do you like football?**
B: If it's a good match, but I'm not that keen. **Actually, I prefer golf myself.**
A: **Do you mean you play golf?**
B: That's right.
A: I play myself. What's your handicap?

12.5
B: Well, Allan, it's getting late. **I have to be off. Thanks for the drink, and good luck with your meeting.**
A: Right, **it was nice talking to you.**
B: **It was nice to meet you too.** Cheerio, then.
A: Bye.

13 Air travel

13.1
A: Good morning.
B: Hello. **Is this where I check in for flight BA 264?**
A: Yes. **Can I see your passport, please?** Thank you. Did you pack your bags yourself, sir?
B: Yes. Excuse me, but apart from my laptop I only have this small bag. Is it okay if I take it on as hand luggage?
A: Well, officially, you're only allowed one piece of hand luggage, but it's not a large bag, is it? So, that's all right, I suppose.
B: Thanks very much. **Could I have an aisle seat, please**, near the front? Or a window seat?
A: I'm sorry, the flight's quite busy. There are no window or aisle seats left.
B: Oh ... **could you show me where the available seats are?**
A: Yes, sir. Here, here and here.
B: Right, I'll take the one up front near the exit on the left.
A: Okay. **Here's your boarding pass.** The flight will be boarding at gate number 23 in 20 minutes. **Have a good flight.**
B: Thanks. Goodbye.
A: Goodbye.

13.2
Book as early as possible – within three weeks of the flight. With an early booking you can choose the seat you want. However, **if you book months in advance, you'll be too early for a seat assignment.**

If you use a travel agent, make sure they have a record of your seating preferences – aisle or window. Tell them you want to sit close to the front. **If you sit at the front, you'll get on and off the plane faster.**

When you receive your ticket and boarding pass or e-ticket confirmation, check the seat assignment. Mistakes happen. **If you have time, cross reference with the airline seating chart.**

If you are unable to confirm a seat, be sure to get to the airport early – at least 45 to 60 minutes before the flight.

If you do have an assignment for your preferred seat, don't check in too late. Those few minutes reading magazines in the newsstand can translate into hours of discomfort in the air.

Finally, the gate check-in attendant can be your best friend. Ask politely if there is a better seat available. Saying that you are claustrophobic might not hurt, but don't feign an illness or say you're pregnant if you're not. There's no point in feeling guilty the entire flight.

If, in spite of your best efforts, you end up with the middle seat, here are some tips to cope:

If you are late boarding and have your choice of middle seats, go for the one up front near the exit.

Check out the aisle and window passengers. Do they look like they will be self-contained and give you plenty of room? Observe their body language and trust your instincts.

Capture as much personal space as you can right away. Dominate the two armrests. This will force your seatmates to give you more space. Be polite, but establish your territory. After all, they have 'personal space' on either side.

Don't work on the laptop during the flight. A cramped space becomes even more claustrophobic when you bring out the hardware. And don't try to read a newspaper. Stick to small paperbacks.

Although it is important to keep hydrated in the air, don't drink water by the gallon. **If you climb over seatmates repeatedly to get to the bathroom, they'll get annoyed.**

Get up once during the flight to stretch your legs. Even if you don't have to use the restroom. This time away will allow your companions to move around as well and refresh the whole row.

13.3
A: If I order 100 units, will you give me a price of 5.5 euros?
B: No, I'm sorry. I can't do that. On 150 units I'll give you a price of six euros.
A: Six euros. And what about payment?
B: Payment is within 60 days.
A: If we pay within 30 days, will you lower the price?
B: I'll go down to 5.5 euros if you order 200 units or more. That's my best offer.
A: Well, what about the guarantee?

14 Hiring and firing

14.1
Speaker 1
I think that these days you have to really sell yourself. Certainly this is what employers expect in the US. You should show them how great and self-confident you are. Modesty isn't going to get you anywhere and no one is going to mind if you exaggerate a bit and dress things up to sound more impressive. Make the potential employer feel that, although this is the job you always wanted and of course you are the ideal person for it, if they don't snap you up, someone else will. So, they had better hire you before they lose the chance.

Speaker 2
It's not often that qualifications and experience totally match up to an advertised post, so it's preferable to emphasise other qualities like your willingness to learn and the fact that you work hard. In fact, you should be careful not to give the impression you are over-qualified for the job. I think that employers are often more interested in things like loyalty and ability to fit in. A high-flier who knows too much can create a bad working atmosphere and break a team. Personally, I want the employer to think that I am going to be easy to work with and won't create too many waves.

Speaker 3
No one likes a 'big head' but, on the other hand, don't be falsely modest either. Basically, your qualifications and experience tell their own story so you're not going to impress anyone by adding a lot of adjectives like 'excellent' and 'outstanding' to your CV. Usually this will make an experienced recruitment officer suspicious. It doesn't hurt to acknowledge one or two weaknesses either – areas that you would like to improve and you want a chance to develop. Above all, be honest, because if you exaggerate or lie, in the end someone is going to catch you out, and you'll end up looking stupid.

Speaker 4
People's motivations interest employers. If you want to work for a specific company, tell them why, especially if you are changing jobs. Valid reasons would be that you are frustrated by the limitations of your present post, or that you can't fulfil the potential of your background and education. Don't whine, though, and don't blame your current employers: you've learnt a lot with them, but it's time to move on. Tell potential employers that you have a lot to offer, and all you need is an opportunity to show it. If someone gives you a break, they won't be disappointed.

14.2
A: Right, shall we make a start? My name is Philip Rickett. I work in the human resources department and I'm responsible for recruitment.
B: Right, pleased to meet you.
A: Did you find us all right?
B: Yes, the map you sent me was very clear.
A: Good. Now, this is just a preliminary interview to check out some details. If you're successful, you'll go on to a more in-depth interview this afternoon. Is that all right?
B: Yes, I don't have to be back at work until tomorrow morning so as long as I have time to drive back this evening, that's fine.
A: Do your present employers know where you are?
B: No. I asked for a day's unpaid leave for personal reasons. I didn't say why.
A: What don't you like about your current position?
B: Actually, there are a lot of things I do like about it, but no job is perfect. I think I am ready for more responsibility and when I saw your advert, I thought I should apply.
A: I see. Well, Sara, can I ask you a few questions about your CV?
B: Sure.
A: You know this job is a managerial position. Do you, in fact, have any managerial experience? It's not very clear from your CV.
B: Well, in my present job I'm a management team co-ordinator.
A: So, you are the manager of a team?
B: Not exactly. I assist the general manager in running the department.
A: In other words, your role is that of a personal assistant?
B: I think it's a bit more than that ...
A: But you personally don't actually have any decision-making power?
B: I suppose not.
A: In your previous position you were an 'SPC professional'. What exactly does that mean? Is Sales Productivity Centre basically a sales department?
B: Yes, we provided backup for twenty salesmen from different sectors of the company.
A: Were you directly involved in sales at all?
B: No, it was more about providing support to help drive sales and increase productivity.
A: I see. So, you were mainly just preparing documentation?
B: Yes, but I would say that it was a position that required a lot of time management skills and prioritising of tasks. It gave me a lot of insight into the sales process.
A: As a department secretary.
B: Not exactly. Okay, some of the work was secretarial but I am applying for your post because I think I am capable of doing far more. I'd like more responsibility and to be able to use my studies and my languages.
A: Yes, your English is obviously excellent and you speak Spanish as well.
B: Yes, it's not bad.
A: Could you tell me about your degree course ... in Spanish?
B: I'm sorry? Oh, I beg your pardon ... Well, I need a little time to think ... Let's see ...

15 Time

15.1
Good morning and welcome. I'm here today to talk about time management. My aim is to share some techniques which will help you to use your time more efficiently.
Time is like money, people and equipment. It's a limited resource. Time management is about making the best possible use of it. So, what are the basic concepts of time management? Today we're going to look at three fundamental steps.

The first step is to analyse how you use your time now.
This requires a methodical approach. Break your day into half hour periods. Record what you do in each period. Look at the list. Ask yourself which tasks were really necessary. Cut everything that isn't necessary. Be ruthless. Most wasted time is the result of unquestioned activity. Take a look at the necessary tasks. Could someone else do them? Never do work yourself that can be safely delegated. Other people may not perform the task as well as you. But without experience they'll never learn.
The next step is to prioritise.
Take the tasks which genuinely require your attention and put them in order of priority – which are the most important, which are urgent needs.
Lastly, organise your time and your tasks.
Ask yourself 'How much time will I need?' Be realistic because work tends to expand to fill the time available.
Set realistic deadlines. The right amount of pressure brings speed and high performance, but on the other hand, too much pressure means things can go wrong.
When possible, organise your work so as to have large blocks of time for top priority tasks like problem analysis and forward planning. Discover the time of day when you are at your best and assign the most difficult tasks to it.
So, analyse, prioritise, organise. Now I'd like to look at what this means in more detail ...

15.2
Conversation 1
A: Where are you going?
B: Well, I've finished everything I had to do so **I'm going to leave early.**
A: What about the sales predictions for next month?
B: Oh, I'd forgotten about that. **I'll start on them tomorrow** first thing. I've arranged to meet someone at five.

Conversation 2
C: Have you planned Mr Logan's visit? What about lunch tomorrow?
D: **I'm going to take him to *The Redwing.***
C: I seem to remember he's a vegetarian.
D: Is he? In that case **I'll phone to check** they have a vegetarian menu.

Conversation 3
E: Is everything confirmed for your trip to San Sebastian?
F: Yes, the plane goes to Bilbao. **I'm going to take the train from there.**
E: No, don't do that – it takes forever. The bus is much faster.
F: Is it? Well, **I'll take the bus**, then.

16 Getting things done

16.1
Conversation 1
A: Oh, look outside!
B: What's up?
A: I've got to go to the Post Office to pick something up and it's raining. **Could you lend me your umbrella?**
B: Of course. **As long as you don't lose it.**
A: Oh, right. Don't worry, I won't.

Conversation 2
C: Gert, I have a meeting with an agent this afternoon, and they're decorating my office.
D: Lucky you.
C: The thing is that I need somewhere quiet where we won't be interrupted. **Could I use your office?**
D: All right, **as long as it's free by four**. I've got a meeting myself.
C: Don't worry, it won't take that long.

16.2
A: Richard, I wonder if I could ask you a favour?
B: Depends what it is.
A: I've got to go over to the warehouse to do something, and I haven't got my car. **Would you lend me yours?**
B: No way!
A: What?
B: I never lend my car! In any case, where's your car?
A: It's in the garage. Eh, I had a little accident.
B: And you expect me to trust you with mine?
A: It's just a minor scratch. **Oh, don't worry. I'll think of something else.**

16.3
A: Sandra, **we need someone to answer the phone from 2.00 til 4.00 while Julia is off sick.** Could you do it?
B: From 2.00 to 4.00? It's not my hours.
A: I know, but you can take the time later on.
B: It's not the time. I'll have to get someone to pick the kids up from school. Isn't there anyone else?
A: No, there isn't. **Look, I know it's inconvenient, but I can't think of any other solution.**
B: Can't we just put the answer phone on for a couple of hours?
A: Not really. It creates such a bad impression. Listen, I'd do it myself but I've got to be somewhere else.
B: I'm sure you would, but it's not my problem, is it?
A: No, it isn't, and **obviously I can't force you to do it, but ...**
B: But?
A: ... but on the other hand, **if you do it, I'll see it as a personal favour.**
B: I see. I don't really have much choice, do I? I hope it's just this time ...
A: Yes, in principle, yes. But you never know. Your contract is up for renewal next month. Enough said?
B: Yeah, enough said.

16.4
Conversation 1
A: Good afternoon, sir.
B: Hello. I'm on flight IB 603. **I was wondering if there's any chance of an upgrade to business class.**
A: Well, I don't know. It depends how crowded the flight is.
B: Yes, **I quite understand, but I'd really appreciate it if you could have a look.** I don't mind paying the extra. It's just that I've had a really hard day and **it'd be really nice to have a bit more space and comfort.**
A: Just a minute, sir.
B: **I'm sorry to put you to any trouble.**
A: No, that's okay. Oh, yes, there's lots of space in business class. I think we can do it.
B: Oh, fantastic. How much is that?
A: That's all right, sir. Don't worry.
B: **Oh, thank you ever so much.**
A: You're welcome. Have a good flight.

Conversation 2
A: Good evening, sir.
B: Look, I'm not at all happy with the room you've given me. It's on the wrong side of the hotel. It faces on to the road and it's far too noisy.
A: I'm sorry, sir. No one has ever said anything before.
B: I can't believe that. Are you going to change it?
A: I don't think I can, sir. We're a bit full tonight.
B: Look, I'm really tired, and the last thing I want to do is argue about my room. If you don't change it, I'll tell my company not to use this hotel again.
A: I'm sorry. There's no other room available.
B: Oh, come on.
A: There's nothing I can do.
B: What about some sort of discount, then?
A: I'm afraid I'm not authorised to offer a discount on your room.
B: So, I have to pay the full price for a noisy room. Brilliant!
A: Sir, if you want, I can call you a taxi ...

17 Office gossip

17.1
A: Hi Quin. How's it going?
B: Trixy! Where have you been?
A: I had a few days' holiday owing to me.
B: Go anywhere interesting?
A: I wish! No, I went up north to stay with my parents.
B: So, you haven't have heard the news.
A: What news?
B: About the 'restructuring'.
A: What restructuring?
B: They want to reorganise marketing and sales.
A: No! Really? Is it official?
B: No, but somebody overheard Prescott talking to one of the management consultants.
A: What did he say?
B: Apparently **he said that we were overstaffed in some areas.**
A: Never!
B: Yes, **this consultant chap told him they would have to let some people go.**
A: But that's awful.
B: Yes, **Prescott asked him how many people it involved.**
A: And what did he say?
B: **He said it depended on individual performance and attitude.**
A: Does that include Maureen?
B: What do you mean?
A: Well, you know what they say about her and Prescott.
B: Go on ...
A: I'm not saying who, but **someone told me he often sees them in *The Green Man* together.**
B: That little pub on the Oxford Road?
A: That's right.
B: Well I never! The other day **he asked her if she would stay behind to work on something together.** I heard him.
A: There you are, then. There's no smoke without fire.
B: Listen, don't tell anyone I told you.
A: Now, come on, Quin, you know me better than that.
B: Back to work, then.
A: Right. Catch you later.
B: Bye.

17.2
Conversation 1
A: Jeff, have you finished last month's production figures?
B: No, Jane, I'm sorry. Can I give them to you this afternoon?
A: It's no good being sorry. There's always some excuse. If they're not on my desk by 4 o'clock, I'll have to speak to Mr Bradley.
B: Yes, Jane. I'll start straight away.

Conversation 2
C: David, have you got a minute? There's something I want to discuss with you ... in my office.
D: What's it about?
C: Oh, well, we're missing a laptop computer from the store.
D: What has that got to do with me?
C: Well, you are the only other person with a key to the store and ...

Conversation 3
E: Marie, the figures you need are ready.
F: Thanks, Pedro. Is everything okay?
E: Yes, no problems. Would you like to look at them with me?
F: Yes, but I'm a bit busy this afternoon.
E: Me too. Er, do you know that new café they've just opened? It's nice and quiet. We can go through them there after work.
F: Oh, I suppose so, but I won't be able to stay for long.
E: Great. See you there at about six, then?
F: Yes, all right. See you there.

Conversation 4

G: Hi, Monica.
H: Oh, hello Jim. How are things going?
G: Great. In fact, you can be the first to congratulate me.
H: Yes, you look very pleased with yourself. What's up?
G: I'm the new head of the eastern sales team.
H: Oh, really? What salary are you on now, then?
G: Sixty grand a year.
H: I can't believe it. Sixty thousand!
G: And they're giving me a new company car.
H: Oh really? Congratulations, then. The drinks are on you. See you later.
G: Yes. Bye.

17.3

A: In this week's *Business Today*, we talk to Karina Schmidt. Karina is the author of a report by the Industrial Society which looks at workplace relations, and how they've changed over the years. Karina, first of all, welcome to the programme.
B: Thank you, it's a pleasure to be here.
A: In your report, you say that many companies nowadays have abandoned some useful institutions which allowed for social interaction.
B: Yes, these days there's less opportunity to gossip and socialise. For example, often the tea trolley has been scrapped, and having a chat in the tea break was an important part of the working day. The drink after work at the pub around the corner is another example.
A: And why do you think these things have disappeared?
B: I think it's all part of the revolution in human resources. Some of these traditions have become unfashionable. Talking about things not connected to work is now seen as bad and as wasting time. There are even theories about removing chairs from meeting rooms, so that the meetings are more efficient and finish quickly.
A: And are we more efficient now, then?
B: Well, that's a good question, but in any case, something has been lost from the workplace which is very important. And perhaps in the long term, with these drives for efficiency, companies are making false economies.
A: In what way?
B: The difference between a good job and a bad job are the human, emotional elements. In other words, happy employees are productive employees. People enjoy the social aspects of work, the personal interaction with colleagues, the friendships ...
A: And the gossip!
B: And the gossip. Yes, in some ways gossip is the glue that holds the organisation together. Providing communal space such as coffee areas or lunch rooms allows employees to share information and build relationships that benefit both the company and the employees.
A: Are you saying that gossip should be encouraged?
B: Not exactly, it's obviously a question of balance. All gossip and chatting doesn't make for an efficient company, but neither does no gossip or chat. All I'm saying is that I think companies would do well to remember this when trying to improve efficiency and bring down costs.
A: Karina, I'm afraid that's all we've got time for. Thank you very much for talking to us. It's been very interesting.
B: Thank you for inviting me.
A: That's all for now from *Business Today*. So, until next week, goodbye.

18 E-commerce

18.1

Lee: There are nearly seven million teenagers in the UK. According to their parents, they wear too much make-up, treat the house like a hotel and run up huge phone bills. **At the same time**, for e-commerce teenagers are a dream because they're so comfortable with the Internet and positive about new technology. And without the financial responsibilites of adults, they generally have money to spend. The sites targeted at these teenagers offer them chat, competitions and e-mail access, as well as things to buy. Lucy, you're the marketing manager of one of these teen sites – Wicked Colours. **How do you see** the future of e-commerce in this market?
Lucy: **I think the main problem is** age. Some sites try to target an age group that's too wide. As a result, they don't satisfy anyone. Some target from 11 to 18-year-olds. But an 11-year-old is nothing like an 18-year-old. We aim our site at younger teenagers. The site is designed for them. The average age would be 13 but we go as young as 11. It's this group that spends the most time at the computer. The 16 to 18-years-olds are interested in other things like going out to clubs. **Would you agree**, Nick?
Nick: **Yes, and the other problem is that** all 13-year-olds want to be 18-year-olds. If you look at the magazines aimed at young teenage girls, most of them have disappeared. The younger kids like to read adult magazines like *Marie Claire* and *Vogue*.
Lee: Okay, **the right audience is one thing, but getting them to buy directly from your site is another**. Most of these sites sell online, but teenagers don't want to ask their parents for their Visa card. Nick?
Nick: **That's right, and** that's why, in my opinion, the teenager market has no future. Apart from the fact that teenagers don't have credit cards, they use the Internet differently from adults. They see it mainly as a means of communication. They will spend hours chatting and sending e-mails – but not shopping. So, you can make some money from advertising, but not much from direct sales. **I think Brian will back me up on that.**
Brian: **Actually, I don't agree**, Nick. Lee is right, they don't want to ask their parents for money every time they want to buy something, but if you free them from that parental control, teenagers will buy online. So, what we do is give them their own magnetic swipe card called *Splash Plastic*. They can use their allowance to top the card up with cash at a number of stores around the country. Then when they're at home, they can use the card to buy online, but only in sites that *Splash Plastic* has authorised as suitable, and only products suitable for under 18-year-olds. In other words, they can't buy X-rated videos. That keeps the parents happy.
Lee: But even if these new payment methods work, isn't there a moral problem? Teenagers make irrational, emotional purchases. So, is it right to market to them so heavily in the first place? Lucy?
Lucy: **Well, that's a good question**, but rightly or wrongly, the current generation of teenagers will have an important influence on the future of e-commerce. It's clear that they want to buy online, and if we don't take advantage of that, someone else will.

18.2

a
The right qualifications for a job **are one thing**, but having experience **is another**.

b
A high turnover **is one thing**, but making good profits **is another**.

c
Having a good idea **is one thing**, but putting it into practice **is another**.

d
High productivity **is one thing**, but improving staff motivation **is another**.

e
Creating a good product **is one thing**, but selling it **is another**.

19 Working from home

19.1

Interview 1

A: The Internet and other new technologies have changed the way we work and the titles of our jobs. For example, instead of the secretary, meet Jill Spencer, a 'virtual assistant'. Jill, what exactly is a virtual assistant?

B: Virtual assistants, or VAs, work from home. We offer services to businesses which don't have sufficient work to justify employing someone full-time.

A: Why did you decide to be a virtual assistant?

B: I retired from my job as a conference organiser, but I wanted to earn some extra money. I became a VA because it meant I didn't have to leave my country home down here in Cornwall.

A: Yes, it's a lovely place – I can understand why you didn't want to move away. So, how did you start?

B: I had a lot of contacts from my previous work. I began by providing things like bookkeeping but now I offer a range of services for clients all over the UK.

A: It's going well, then.

B: Yes, I wasn't looking to earn a fantastic amount of money. The biggest advantage is that you can do as little or as much as you want. If it's a lovely sunny day, I can sit out in the garden and do the work in the evening.

A: What do you need to get started?

B: The basic tools are a computer with an Internet connection, a fax machine and a mobile phone. Anyone with basic office skills could do the job. Apart from that it depends on the kind of services you're going to offer and what the clients want.

A: And what's in it for the companies?

B: Companies get a huge amount out of it because they only use a virtual assistant when they need one. Also, they can perhaps get someone with a higher professional level than they could get if they had to pay someone full-time. There's also no problem of office hours. A businessman can be out of the office all day, but his assistant is still available in the evening if he needs to discuss things. I think it could make a big difference to everyone's lifestyle.

Interview 2

A: Anna, what exactly do you do?

B: I'm a concierge at the Westin Hotel in Santa Clara, California.

A: What was life like before you became a teleworker?

B: I had to get up at three in the morning so I could shower and dress, take my kids to my mother's, and set off to work by 4.30.

A: 4.30!

B: Yes, there was a lot of traffic. On a good day I got there by 6.30. That gave me half an hour to relax before starting my shift at seven o'clock.

A: It sounds awful.

B: Yes, I was getting up in the dark and getting home in the dark. I never saw my husband or children. I like my job but my life was a nightmare.

A: And what is life like now?

B: Oh, I feel like the luckiest person alive. I now get up at 5.30. My mother still looks after the children but I don't have the 80-mile drive to work along Highway 101. We've set up my workplace in one of the bedrooms. I sit down in front of a camera, pin on a microphone and I'm ready for business.

A: How does it work at the hotel?

B: Guests still go up to the concierge desk, but instead of me in person, they see me on a giant TV screen. They can only see my head and shoulders, so I can wear my slippers while I work.

A: What do your employers think about it?

B: Oh, they're happy because they can't afford to lose me. In the hotel industry we don't have the high salaries of Cisco, Palm or Sun Micro, so there's a high turnover of staff. With unemployment around here so low it's hard to replace workers. It cost them $50,000 but they thought it was worth a try.

A: And the guests?

B: They're happy. Apart from anything else they don't have to leave a tip!

20 Working lunch

20.1

A: **This looks like a very nice place**, Satoshi.

B: Yes, **I thought you would like it.**

A: Yes, **I really like the decor**. Er, **could you order for both of us**, Satoshi?

B: Of course. **I think we could have some miso soup to start with.** They do it very well here.

A: Okay. **Sounds good.**

B: And then **I think you should try some *unagi*.**

A: What's that?

B: It's eel – grilled and served on a bed of rice. It's delicious.

A: Hm, I'm sure it is. Actually, **do you think I could have a steak?**

B: Well, **I'm afraid they don't serve steak here.**

A: **I'll try the *unagi*, then**.

B: Fine. **Would you like some sake, or would you prefer some beer?**

A: No, no, **let's have some sake.**

B: Right. **Sake it is, then.**

20.2

B: Neil, I met Jeff Segram earlier this year. **What exactly is his job title?**

A: He's the Managing Director.

B: **Do you mean the CEO?**

A: Yes, that's what the Americans say. **He's the person on the board who is responsible for the day to day running of the company.**

B: And what about you?

A: I'm the Product Development Director. I'm on the board as well, but **I report to Jeff.**

B: Right, I see.

20.3

C: So, any news from Tokyo, Neil?

A: No, I'm afraid not, Jeff. It looks like they're not interested.

C: **How did it go with Mr Tanaka?**

A: Oh, he was really nice. He took me to a great restaurant. Actually, everything went okay until we got down to business.

C: **What happened?**

A: I don't know. I thought the sale was a sure thing, but he seemed to lose interest. I don't know what I did wrong.

20.4

A: Mm, **that was delicious.**

B: **I'm glad you enjoyed it.** So, Neil, tell me about this digital control software. Why do you think we should be interested?

A: Because it's easily the best program for the job on the market.

B: The system we use at the moment works okay. Why should we change?

A: It's a question of costs. It could save you up to 30%. If you look at the competition, there's just no comparison.

B: Can you give me some information about your sales?

A: Er ... about two million dollars worth worldwide.

B: Could I see the documentation?

A: Well, I'm afraid that's confidential, but listen, if we can make a deal today, I can offer you an even better discount.

Macmillan Education
Between Towns Road, Oxford OX4 3PP
A division of Macmillan Publishers Limited
Companies and representatives throughout the world

ISBN 0 333 95726 1

Text © Simon Clarke 2003
Design and illustration © Macmillan Publishers Limited 2003

First published 2003

All rights reserved; no part of this publication may be reproduced, stored in a retrieval system, transmitted in any form, or by any means, electronic, mechanical, photocopying, recording, or otherwise, without the prior written permission of the publishers.

Designed by Jackie Hill at 320 Design
Illustrated by Mike Stones icon research photos Photodisc; Cyrus Deboo pp26, 58; Max Ellis p7; Julian Mosedale pp31, 57, 69, 78
Cover design by Jackie Hill at 320 Design
Cover illustration by Mike Stones research photos Photodisc
Photo research by Sally Neal

Author's acknowledgements:
When David Riley from Macmillan contacted me about this project, writing a book was really the last thing I had on my mind. I was quite happy with my placid existence in the green hills of the Basque Country in northern Spain, and had no real desire to get involved in such a daunting and challenging project. (I've always thought that 'challenging' basically means something difficult, stressful and probably vaguely unpleasant.) In the end, my decision to accept the proposal had more to do with divine intervention than David's legendary powers of persuasion. By chance, soon after that initial phone call, I broke my wrist in a cycling accident. What does a confirmed cycling addict do during the eight or nine weeks of wearing a heavy plaster cast while the delicate scaffold bone slowly heals? Suddenly, it seemed that as I was obliged to sacrifice my daily mileage fix, I would have time on my hands and I should have a go. So, if my life has been ruined, it wasn't entirely David's fault, it was mainly God's. In any case, thanks to David for thinking of me. His advice and guidance throughout the editing process have been fundamental and I am indebted to him for the ideas and suggestions he passed my way.

The person on the Macmillan team who has had to put up with me most has been Erika Vivers, the managing editor. I can only say that she has been fantastic. It has been a real pleasure to work with someone so talented and professional, as well as consistently supportive, good-humoured and encouraging. Thanks also to Jackie Hill and the rest of the design team for doing such a fine job in bringing the text to life.

For the last 17 years I have worked for Academia Lacunza – International House San Sebastian. Had I worked elsewhere, I might well not have had so many opportunities for development as a teacher and materials writer. I would particularly like to mention my colleague and coauthor on previous projects, John Bradley, who is a continual source of inspiration and ideas, and the director of the school, Javier Lacunza, who also offered encouragement and support. My thanks, too, to Chris Monk, who piloted material and provided useful feedback.

Last but not least, my family have had to put up with me while I was working on the book, so thanks to them for letting me get on with the job, and understanding that I couldn't be with them as much as I should have been.

The publishers would like to thank Bob Ratto, Byron, Rome; Angela Wright, British Council, Rome; Norman Cain, IH Rome; Fiona Campbell, Teach-In, Rome; Sue Garton, Lois Clegg and Irene Frederick, University of Parma; Simon Hopson and Gordon Doyle, Intensive Business English, Milan; Dennis Marino, Bocconi University, Milan; Mike Cruikshank, Advanced Language Services, Milan; Christine Zambon, Person to Person, Milan; Fiona O'Connor, In-Company English, Milan; Peter Panton, Panton School, Milan; Colin Irving Bell, Novara; Marta Rodriguez Casal, Goal Rush Institute, Buenos Aires; Elizabeth Mangi and Silvia Ventura, NET New English Training, Buenos Aires; Graciela Yohma and Veronica Cenini, CABSI, Buenos Aires; Viviana Pisani, Asociación Ex Alumnos, Buenos Aires; Claudia Siciliano, LEA Institute, Buenos Aires; Cuca Martocq, AACI, Buenos Aires; Laura Lewin, ABS International, Buenos Aires; Charlie Lopez, Instituto Big Ben, Buenos Aires; Alice Elvira Machado, Patricia Blower; Valeria Siniscalchi; Carla Chaves; Virginia Garcia; Cultura Inglesa, Rio de Janeiro; Susan Dianne Mace, Britannia, Rio de Janeiro; John Paraskou, Diamond School, Sèvres; Dorothy Polley and Nadia Fairbrother, Executive Language Services, Paris; Claire MacMurray, Formalangues, Paris; Claire Oldmeadow, Franco British Chamber of Commerce, Paris; Ingrid Foussat and Anne James, IFG Langues, Paris; Karl Willems, Quai d'Orsay Language Centre, Paris; Louis Brazier, Clare Davis, Jacqueline Deubel, Siobhan Mlačak and Redge, Télélangue, Paris; John Morrison Milne, Ian Stride, Gareth East and Richard Marrison, IH Madrid; Gina Cuciniello; Helena Gomm; Paulette McKean.

The authors and publishers would like to thank the following for permission to reproduce their material:
Adapted extract from 'Customised Greetings Cards Win Stamp of Approval' from *The Times* 16.12.00 copyright © NI Syndication Limited, London 2000, reprinted by permission of the publisher; Adapted extract from www.betterdogfood.com, reprinted by permission of the publisher; Adapted extract from 'Ringing Up The Millions' from www.brendan.com.au, reprinted by permission of Brendan Walsh; Adapted extract from 'Hotels Play the Global Brand Game' by Andrew Clark 18.04.01 from www.guardian.co.uk/Archive/Article/0,4273,4171589,00.html, copyright © The Guardian 2001, reprinted by permission of the publisher; Adapted extract from 'The 50 Richest in the World' from *Forbes 400* October 2001 and *Forbes Global* March 2002, copyright © Forbes Inc 2002, reprinted by permission of Forbes Magazine; Adapted extract from 'The Worm Man' by Lee Stokes from *BMG Online Magazine* www.bmgroup.co.uk, reprinted by permission of the author; Adapted extracts and photograph from www.inditex.com/english/home.htm, reprinted by permission of the publisher; Adapted extract from 'Wasting Time at Work' by Galen Black from www.vgg.com, reprinted by permission of The Van Gogh-Goghs: www.vgg.com; Dictionary extracts from the Macmillan English Dictionary © Bloomsbury Publishing Plc 2002.

Whilst every effort has been made to trace owners of copyright material in this book, there may have been some cases when the publishers have been unable to contact the owners. We should be grateful to hear from anyone who recognises copyright material and who is unacknowledged. We shall be pleased to make the necessary amendments in future editions of the book.

The authors and publishers would like to thank the following for permission to reproduce their photographs:
Action Plus/S.Bardens p13; Alamy/P.Bowater p5(m), ImageState p12, C.Newham p33(mb), C.Lewis p38, Novastock p45(b), A.Willett p49(t), T.Tracy p58, R.F p64(t), Rubberball p75, ImageState p83, R.F p85, H.Sieplinga p87; Car Photo Library/D.Kimber p35(b); Cartoonbank/M.Maslin p8; Cartoon Stock/C.Zahn p117, J.Morris p119; Corbis/J.L.Pelaez p4, T.Horowitz p23(t), W.Tenaillon p23(b), Sygma/D.Lamont p51, R.W.Jones p66(t), L.Bonaventure p66(b); Eyewire p91; Farabolafoto p67; Getty/H.Kingsnorth pp10, 89(mb), B.Bailey p14, K.Mori p17(rt), B.Truslow p17(rb), R.Chapple pp17(b), 45(mb), C.Bissell p20, X. Bonghi p21, M.Douet p32(t), R.Lockyer p32(b), P.Eckersley p33(mt), P.Turner p33(b), K.Chiba p34, J.L.Batt p39, M.Goldman p40(l), C.Franklin p40(m), Chabruken p40(r), K.Biggs p42(t), T.Anderson p45(mt), M.Douet p53, B.Ayers p56, D.Roth p64(mt), China Tourism Press p64(mb), D.Robb pp64(b), 89(t), T.Brown p65, B.Erlanson p72, J.Bradley p77, P.Scholey p81, S.Hunt p86, E.Dryer p88, G.Wade p89(mt), J.Tisne p89(b), P.Arthur p90, C.Simmons p93; Foodpix p33(t); Hulton Archive/T.Hopkins p28, J.Kobal p52, Hulton Archive pp37, 47, 70; ImageState pp9(t), 15, 45(t), 46, Inditex pp42(b), 43; Maserati/PFPR p35(t); Moonpig p5(t), P.A p24; New Yorker/© 2002 The New Yorker Collection from cartoonbank.com. All Rights Reserved; Photodisc p46, 61; Powerstock pp9(b), 29, 60, 63; Private Eye/K.Smith p27; Remote Lounge/J.Cate p54; Science Photo Library/Tek Image p5(b); Sporting Pictures/P.O'Connor p49(b); Topham/A.P p25, Photri p55; Vin Mag Archive p73.

Printed and bound in Spain by Edelvives SA

2007 2006 2005 2004 2003
10 9 8 7 6 5 4 3